Father Ahavah:

The Unfathered Ones Come Home to Love

Dr. Ann Marie Nielsen, Ph.D.

Father Ahavah™

Copyright © 2015-Present, Ann Marie Nielsen, Ph.D.

Dr. Ann Marie Nielsen has asserted her right under the Copyright, Designs, and Patent Act, 1988, to be identified as the author of this work. All rights reserved.

No part of this book may be reproduced, or utilized in any form or by any means, electronic or mechanical, without prior permission in writing from Dr. Ann Marie Nielsen.

The Nameless Speaks Publications

United States of America

ISBN: 978-0-9975228-0-8

I Have Loved You With an Everlasting Love (Ahavah)

(Jeremiah 31:3).

The Hebrew spelling of Ahavah (Love)

Dr. Ann Marie Nielsen
The Author

Ann Marie Nielsen, Ph.D. serves as an Author, Visionary, Audio/Video Presenter & Creator, Seminar & Retreat Leader, *Home in the Heart Foundation* Founder & President, Public Speaker, Spiritual Mentor, Consultant, Licensed Mental Health Counselor FL 8181, Licensed Pastoral Counselor, Life Wellness Center Owner.

And One
Who Has Deep Compassion
For Humanity

And Who Sees

We Are
Still
Home

Still One

With Father Ahavah

Home in the Heart Family & Foundation

Home in the Heart is more than a book series. *Father Ahavah* is more than a book.

The message of *Father Ahavah reveals* a way of life. It opens pathways of *being*.

Dr. Nielsen, *Home in the Heart,* and *Father Ahavah* messages, offer a rare depth of wisdom, compassion, and support for our family and followers. We offer books, audios, online discourse programs, classes, articles, support messages, retreats, and individual consultations.

We see you as a sacred gift and we are dedicated to serving and supporting you in a multitude of ways.

In addition, we gratefully receive your prayer and monetary support for the furtherance of the ministry. The investment of your Presence and sharing of resources strengthens this outreach nationally and globally. As you flourish in loving spiritual life, you simultaneously support all beings in doing so.

For More Upcoming Books, Audios, Classes Visit:
drannmarie.com

For Upcoming Courses in the Online Classroom:
homeintheheart.com

For Information on Home in the Heart Foundation Visit:
homeintheheartfoundation.com

Home in the Heart Foundation is a 501(c)(3) tax deductible, non-profit organization, dedicated to charitable contribution to humanity's peace, flourishing, and spiritual awareness. *Home in the Heart Foundation* distributes copies of this book to churches and to organizations that support spiritual life, healing from trauma and abuse, recovery from PTSD, and such. The *Foundation* reaches people locally, nationally, and internationally.

We Welcome You To The Home in the Heart Family

A Portion of the Proceeds of this Book Supports Charitable Organizations & Purposes

Is This a True Story?

The initial writing of this book flowed quickly, spontaneously, effortlessly.

Every memory, nuance, thought, and emotion of the vignettes sprang forth, as if happening afresh, a moment ago. The experiential contemplations and prayers, the wisdom messages of many years, flowed as if vibrantly fresh and new that instant.

These life events occurred in this world.

Yet the real question is, are life events real? Are they true?

At the sensory, mental, emotional level—the level of the "movie" that you experience as your life—yes, they are real.

However, at a deeper level, at the core of our being, at an existential spiritual level, they are not the ultimate truth.

One definition of the "true," of the "real," is that which does not change, that which is permanent, that which is eternal.

That which is temporal, changing, subject to the pairs of opposites, labeled as "good" and "bad," permeated with a separate sense of a "personal me," is not the core of truth.

What is true, everlasting and changeless is that we exist as *Spirit Life*. As *Spirit Life* we exist as *Happiness, as Peace, as Light,* as *One with God, as Presence*. This is our ultimate truth.

All else is story, is character, is temporal.

Yet the temporal story allows us to see what happens when we perceive ourselves as separate from sacredness, from holiness, from *God... Presence... Oneness*. We sense the hollowness of the temporary and feel homesick for *Home*.

We experience fear, contraction, limitation, or suffering. And with the wisdom and contemplative practices that spark flashes of freedom, our eyes open to see how to set patterns down, like an outdated old piece of jewelry. On one level, it's that simple.

We see, *Oh, this is not what I wish to create, not the ultimate truth of "me."* And we see, *Oh, I now remember Home, remember sacredness, remember changeless happiness, remember the reality of existence as one with God Presence.* And finally we see, *Oh, there is no personal me who wakes up and "becomes" spirit. Spirit Is, and I Am that* —One with Father Ahavah!.

In the beginning... God.

And God is Light...

And in this simplicity, we remember *Home*.

Home is Oneness with *"God Is."*

Home is the natural way, the essence of heaven. God Presence is Light. God Presence is Eternal and Immortal Life—*Living, Alive*.

Thus, God Presence is Living, Eternal Light.

We are created in the image and likeness of *That*...as our *Spirit Self*, our true *Home*.

Home is *Spirit, the Original Self, One with God,* before thought, before time, before limitation of any kind. *Home* is the remembrance of *Divine Love.*

At times it may not seem that simple or that easy. It is simple. However, "simple" does not mean superficial, shallow, or a quick fix. It takes a true depth of humility, surrender, and dedication to remember *Home.* More than anything, it takes total adoration of the *Divine Presence.*

As we remember this *Spirit Presence,* in limitless *Grace*—it then informs and forms our world as the light of that world.

That is what is true.

Allow this "true" separation story that follows, to spark a remembrance of the more deep and "true real story" of the reality of *Home, in God.* Abide as that *Holy Presence,* here now, that is beyond all stories, all persons, all situations.

Allow the suffering and trauma of the human drama, to engender a passion to awaken to the Spirit Oneness beyond all pressured duress and all primal agonies.

This *Home is* not a place or a person; it is *Eternal Father God.*

Ineffable Endless Love.

And it is the Real Self, already limitless, already all love, already one with *God Light.*

Still Home.

Still Father Ahavah - Eternal Father Love!

Welcome Home

Come Home

Still Home

Home

Prelude:

The Heart of the Father: The Global Condition & The Return Home

This is not intended as a story of a girl abused by her father, or alone in the world. This is not intended as a story of blame or accusation.

This tells *the* story about *"the pain."* It depicts the collective virus of forgetfulness. This is what humans do to each other, what we do to ourselves, when we *forget*.

This goes far beyond what "my" father did or did not do. It reaches beyond what I did or did not do. It does not aim to describe certain individual people. The message reveals globally ingrained human patterns and beliefs... the existential pain we all feel when we identify as a personal "me" apart from *Spirit Light*.

This story awakens us from the amnesia of sleep, and redeems us from the avalanche of trivia and denial. Then we may truly see, hear, touch, and experience what happens when we *forget* we exist as one with the *Divine, as Spirit Presence, as the Eternal Way.*

We now stand on the precipice of an en masse emergence of the eternality of the heart.

We embody this *Eternal Love* when we come *Home in the Heart.* And we rest in this reality of inner love again and again, no matter how messy the moments, or crucial the challenges we face.

This one-by-one perpetual intelligent luminosity of being *Still Home,* moves us toward a collective shift to *Father Ahavah!* the heart of the *Divine Father Spirit Love.* This epic hour of astounding Grace heralds the miracles of compassion, the beholding of ecstatic holiness.

Felt now.

This message reveals the longing we share for the *Father's Love.* Ultimately this *Father must* go beyond a human person, or gender; it *must* go beyond an object, or something seen as external or personal.

This *Father Ahavah* is known as *Primordial,* as *Eternal,* as the *One God.*

And yet this *Father Spirit,* this *Father Heart,* this *Father God Light is within us — is us, as us.* Like the ray of the sunbeam streams as one with the sun, or the wave flows as one with the ocean, we are *so one* with this Spirit Presence — we *are* this.

We feel this *Presence* happening on the "inside" and then we reveal this to all on earth.

And in knowing this *Father Ahavah*, this Heart of the Father God, we know the Heart of the Mother, the Anointed Compassionate One, prior to suffering, duality or lack.

And we come *Home to this... as Self.*

It is the *Prior To Self.*

We exist as this Light, prior to our father relationship, prior to and beyond any relationship, prior to a personal "me" who feels separate from the eternal truth.

This moves us far beyond a book about trauma and pain. It's potent message opens the pathway of direct revelation of the *Spirit Life, Presence,* as more real than trials and trauma.

This does not intend to portray one person as guilty and another as innocent. It highlights the suppressed subtle anxieties and the poignant primal agonies we endure when we feel separate from the true life spring of Divinity.

Father Ahavah ushers in the return *Home* to the *Heart of the Father,* the Light of Original Oneness. This message heralds a call to Eternal Innocence.

This message gently guides us toward humility, sincerity, and an honoring of the sacred.

It restores the innate reverence of the *Divine Feminine.*

This book illumines the tangible, practical, expression of the *Prior To Light*—the light of the world—prior to the world and beyond it. It is *Prior To,* any sense of separation, any conditioning or any limitation.

This book is an experiential writing—a direct shift of tangible experience—to the deep reality of *Father Ahavah*, the Divine Presence.

It is the actual direct experience of you prospering as the *Unconditional Happiness of our Holy Father,* prior to daughters, or sons, or fathers.

Father Ahavah!

Father Ahavah

Direct Experience:

How to Benefit the Most From This Book

The book *Father Ahavah* is *experiential reading*.

Meaning: the book has the capacity to deliver the actual experience of what you read. As you read, and absorb the message, it supports lasting benefits within you.

You may instantaneously and spontaneously experience spiritual realizations and ease of suffering. You may feel this immediately, or you may notice over the upcoming days, weeks, or months that you feel lighter, spacious, and free.

You will benefit the most from this book by *resting and relaxing into it*. Rest from any mental strain, or any attempt to learn. Rather than learning, this presents an opportunity for unlearning. Unlearn the past. Unlearn past conditioning. Unlearn a limited identity. Unlearn separation.

Rather than struggling with mental concepts, feel the essence of the message wash over you, as if luxuriating in a warm, soothing bath. In a nurturing bathing experience, you immerse yourself in that which cleanses, uplifts, revitalizes you. You don't figure the bath out; you simply experience it.

Simply experience *Father Ahavah*.

Open to a sacred devotion and adoration to and from the Divine Father God that created you as Spirit Light.

If a word or phrase appears that you have not heard before, and after opening to the essence of the phrase you still remain curious, you may refer to the glossary in the back of the book.

Before reading each chapter or each chapter section, pause for a moment. Take a few deep breaths. And allow this time for *you*. Let go of any worry or problems, concerns of the past, or anxieties of the future. Release attention to anyone or anything else. Allow this to be *your gift to you, the Eternal One's gift to you* — to simply *be with* this *Father Ahavah Presence* and message.

As you read, relax and center yourself in each present moment. Open to release all past pain. Allow pain you have held inside to be cleansed and washed away through this reading. If the vignettes spark buried hurts, engage a support system or loving friends and family, or caring counsel to stand beside you.

As you read, release attachment to a personal "me." And rest in remembrance of the Real Self you exist as… *Home… one with God Presence*, alive as that ecstatic holiness of nascent joy.

The book <u>*intentionally repeats*</u> key themes and phrases. See the repetition as similar to inhaling the fragrance of a rose again and again, receiving a more rich and refined perfume of peace each time you inhale the delicious and inviting beauty of truth.

Father Ahavah is a unique phrase, offered by Dr. Nielsen in contemplation and teaching. The Father relates to *the Eternal Father*. Yet it also connotes the *Original Divine Light*, our *Beloved Supreme Ineffable Creator*.

Ahavah is the Hebrew word for *Love*. We find this elegant word in ancient scriptures to describe the everlasting Love of God. In Hebrew, a word carries the vibrational essence of its meaning. *To say or think, or contemplate Ahavah, is to feel Love, be Love.*

The more you read and experience the book, the more that the mere contemplation of *Father Ahavah* deepens the transformative intimate communion.

As you read, pause often and rest deeply in the heart as *Father Ahavah!*

As you move through your day and feel a peaceful joy: pause and allow it to deepen in *Father Ahavah*.

When encountering a challenge, suffering, or pain, simply stop for a moment. And allow your whole being to relax and surrender into the nurturing, strengthening, powerful reality of Father Ahavah.

The Wider View
How to Not Miss The Impact of This Book

If you read this as a story about a woman, and the things she "learned", you have missed this book.

The vignettes break through the fog of amnesia to reveal poignantly: *the condition.*

This does not describe one woman's plight... rather, it reveals *the condition*... the en masse matrix of pain... appearing in multitudes who forgot their true nature.

We unwittingly abandon ourselves, and each other, settling for the superficial, the hollow, and the fake— if we live from an identity other than *Spirit, One with Creator.*

I received word last week of a Catholic priest crucified... in 2016...

I consulted many beings this past week, broken hearted— treated as insignificant to their partners.... emotionally crucified... in 2016...

First we get real and candid, honest... truly honest... honest enough to come out of game playing and hiding... and *see the condition*, the suffering.

And we then allow the passion to increase for true answers, for intimate union with Eternal Love.

The *Now* and *Experiential Application* sections of the book, and the later chapters, offer pathways of *Home* and foundations to live the *real* in this context of the make-believe *lost* world.

Rather than seeing this book as about one person... or a few persons... and missing its influence and impact, see it as a *Light Trigger*, to face the condition as un-anesthetized and alive as the *Sacred Immensity of God Presence*.

This book is impersonal, not personal.

It bears similarity to *Somewhere Over the Rainbow*. The song speaks of and carries the lower tones of the aching, the longing that we share. Then the song hits the high note, rises to the rainbow, and *over* the rainbow, way up *high*.

The *Then* section vignettes reveal the low note, the en masse longing, the sense of separation. And the *Now* and *Experiential Applications* hit the high C, the high notes, the celestial tone.

However in the *Wizard of Oz*, the real world happens in Kansas. In this book the real world is the golden world of *Light*. More specifically, the real world reflects ineffable *Divine Love in the kingdom inside*.

God Presence.

To truly receive the impact of this book, first open to see and feel, *the condition*.

And allow that to spark total passion for total reverence and remembrance.

A conviction.

This illumines the innate devotion to the *Real* so deeply and potently, we live it even here.

Allow this book to awaken a *Coming Home to Father Ahavah!*

Chapter Contents

1. *The Freeze*: From the Blows That Freeze to the Freedom of Sacredness Accepted

    Experiential Application: *The Presence Only Love Is: Dissolving Trauma Memories, Restoring Calm Presence*

2. *The Swallow*: From The Swallowing Truth to Being Heard as Divine Voice

    Experiential Application: *I Am the Voice That Remembers Home, Born of Divinity*

3. *The Wall*: From The Wall To Heaven's Immortal Wings

    Experiential Application: *I Speak With Immortality's Lungs And Soft Fires Of Heaven's Voice*

4. *Forgotten*: From the Unconsciousness That Numbs, To Self-Complete Happiness

    Experiential Application: *I Exist As The Sacred Immensity Without Walls, Immortal Lung's of Heaven's Voice as Self Complete Happiness Presence*

5. *Lost:* From I Lost What I Was, To Glorious Ineffable Essential Purpose

    Experiential Application: Alive as *Self Complete Happiness Presence*

6. *The Initiation:* From Initiation Into Violence, To the Power of the *Quieting*

    Experiential Application: *The Eternal Power of The Quieting*

7. *The Tap*: From Domination's Crushing To The Wings of The Free

   Experiential Application: *The Glory of the Wings, The Divine Papa Tenderness That Births The Limitless*

8. *The Vulnerability:* From The Vulnerable One To The Feminine Redeemed As Light & Peace

   Experiential Application: *Light & Peace, Feminine / Masculine Kindness As One*

9. *The Jolt:* From Jammies Shocks To The Time When All Was Kind

10. *How to Honor Our Dads and Be the Father Heart*

11. *The Return of the Heart of the Father*

12. *Fathers Provoke Not Your Children to Wrath*: Daughters and Sons Live as Courageousness Innocence

    Experiential Application: *Live as the Courageous Innocence*

13. *"I Want A Daddy So Badly"*

    Experiential Application: Dissolve: *"I Want a Daddy So Badly": Abide As Story Free Self-Completion*

14. *The Power of Dissolving the Polarity*

    Experiential Application: *Polarity Process*

15. *Wake Up! The Dream-Like Movie*

16. *Embracing:* Prior to Daddy: The Feminine Light

    Prior to the Feminine Light: *Father Ahavah*

17. *The Power of the Prior To*

18. *Giving Birth:* The Daughter of the Fire as the Heart of the Father

19. *Pruning:* Or The Divine Shattering Open In Light?

Chapter One

The Freeze

From the Blows That Freeze
To The Freedom of Sacredness Accepted

Then

The freeze.

It happened so quickly, there was no way to move.

No way to run... nowhere to hide... no time to even put up a hand or an arm.

No protective embrace, no familiar face, no place…

No one.

Nowhere.

My living, breathing, female body of flexible flesh and bones became frozen in time, petrified wood, unable to move. The time from **Dad a few feet away** to **Dad's rage all over me and within me**, was a split nanosecond, a lightning-fast trauma flash.

The frightening fury on his face, the hardened hatred in his intention, the determined drive to punish, the subtle surprising haunting fear in the eyes, all registered as "I wish this child would die."

My infraction: *I was too loud.*

Dad's embarrassingly young wife—who had replaced me as "Daddy's girl"— was inconvenienced. She wished to go to sleep early, so she could get up and enjoy her morning coffee before she went to work cutting hair.

I was an introverted, quiet straight A student. But I was "too loud." And for this, I encountered *The Shattering: the annihilation of the integrity of my self and the shaking to the core of the precious being I hoped I was.*

I thought I stayed quiet enough. Nonetheless...

Like a boxer, Dad swung his interlocked hands with full-body force onto my fourteen-year-old head.

With each physical blow, his words stung like acid rain—a river of hatred—searing rejection deep into my tender heart, worthlessness into my blood, and invalidation into my bones: "I hate you! You will go to school in rags! You will live in isolation in your room!"

Lying alone in bed that night, I trembled as hot tears cascaded over my aching cheeks. Darkness descended like a heavy cloak of tar that constricted my chest, and my lungs filled with too many microtears to fully breathe.

My heart closed tighter and tighter around its treasures, which now seemed smaller and smaller, and less and less significant.

My head throbbed with searing pain as the knife-sharp words replayed on and on.

An unmovable stone lodged in the pit of my throat.

That night the last vestiges of my angel-winged hopes—flying high for Daddy's love—died. The wings, clipped off, fell to the ground. Only the shame was deathless.

Only shame was.

Shame: the companion. I could say *"I love me"* a million times like a sacred prayer, like a mantra, but my frail words bounced off the imprint cemented within: my father *hates me.*

Ashamed. Worthless. Unloved.

My body went into neurological alert. Watching, waiting. Tired, so tired. No comfort remained in my troubled, vulnerable home of a body.

Several weeks later I writhed on the floor in pain. Admitted to the hospital for codeine injections, I cringed at questions from medical staff. By then, no external injuries were visible. No tests were conducted. The doctors and nurses asked if I knew what may cause such head pain.

The shame and fear of telling on my own father shot up so strongly, that I felt nauseous. I choked out: *School stress. I am studying so hard, so worried about my grades.* It was not the last codeine injection for "school stress."

The emotional pain of the knowing that *I am hated*—of my defeat to win father's love—went on for years. And not hated by a convict, or a jealous peer, or a gang down the street, but passionately hated, *by my own father, my* **dad**, whom I loved more than anyone in the world.

I so, so, badly wanted him to be my daddy. *I wanted a Real Father!*

I had tried again and again to have a close relationship with my father.

Years earlier as a little girl, every day I watched for him to come home. I loyally prepared a picture, a snack, a poem... *some little something,* just for him.

I felt proud on *Dad's Day* visits in third grade at elementary school. Even though the lunch tasted like cardboard and glue, when Dad said "You eat like kings here," my hazel eyes opened wide and I exclaimed, "We do?!"

When eight years old, I came home to a note on my pink gingham bedspread. He was *gone*. Dad no longer came home for my little hugs or big attempts at brownies. His focus now divided with new priorities, my father turned into a more distant masculine influence. I grieved, dejected and sullen.

When I missed him, I made up math problems as an excuse to call him on the phone. Long after I solved the problem, I pretended not to know the answer, just to keep him on the phone a little longer.

When I did spend time with my father, I felt the stress of how his new relationship strained our interactions. His primary attention gravitated to his new life with the new daddy's girl—his young girlfriend. She competed with me for his attention, and won.

Being my father's priority was not a birthright gift freely offered, upon which I could depend and trust. The stress of his absence, along with his verbal criticism and physical violence, spiraled my emotional life into repetitive cycles of anxiety and instability.

Being his priority, or even truly feeling like *his*, like *"his* daughter," drifted away like a distant ship on blue seas—it sails so far over the amber horizon that it disappears into a gray fog. I progressively lost the battle for significance, until I felt the empty futility of chasing his staccato affection.

In my life, my father stood as the prime masculine authority, the strong mirror, who reflected back to me who I *was*, my *value*, the meaning of my existence—as a girl, and later as a woman. The father reveals to us if we are loved, if we are worthy, if we are precious, if we are beautiful... or NOT.

After years of rejection, the physical abuse—the blows to my head—and "I hate you" at age fourteen signaled my final and irreparable defeat.

I felt... I am not! Not loved, not worthy, not precious, not beautiful.

After the blows of that night, I felt ugly.

A deep shame, ugliness. So, so ugly.

I faltered in expressing my true feelings, speaking up, or making a stand with others. I ached to feel esteemed, safe and embraced with kindness. The rejection, replayed like an unremitting chilling life sentence. At times in this world I felt a questioning quiet desperation, born of an inner quivering agony. This spurred an inner quest for truth and freedom.

What is love?

Who am I?

Why am I here?

Where is God?

For years, the emotional wounds persisted and true healing remained elusive. Every morning I awoke to the depression-as-companion, voicing the "I don't want to be here like this" anymore.

By my teens, I lived full time with my father and stepmother. I alternated between withdrawing in isolation in my room, and going out for hours by myself. Anywhere—from long walks along the ocean to riding the circuits of the city bus—I'd go anywhere to get out of the house for a while.

Nowhere felt truly safe to my heart.

All trust, *the trust of what was on the outside, and the trust of what was on the inside,* had been shattered.

Only one thing kept the young "me" alive. That final blow—on top of innumerable other assaults on my body, emotions and esteem—rendered it impossible to go on with this pain without a miracle. Only the riveting glimpses of union with the *Creator*, beyond this world, kept the flickering flame of *the will to live* alive.

In this vulnerable age of the first budding of womanhood, I quietly pondered, "I will not survive unless I *deeply know and feel God... as love... on the inside... all the time.*"

I knew that *God, Spirit, Presence, Light could not be a concept*—God had to be REAL.

And I knew that God had to be *more real to* me than the trauma, than this world. The *Light, the Love,* had to be *more real* than the darkness. My whole being had to intimately know *Eternal Father* as the *Reality* in an unshakably relevant and sustained way.

I clearly remember thinking about the abuse: "This is not God. This cannot be God."

Now

If our parents—our initial caregivers—reject us, if they withhold their love, if they do not respond to our heart's request to be seen, nurtured, protected, fully accepted, and loved unconditionally, then we feel LOST. We learn early that *we are unlovable*, and this belief is imprinted in our heart. And if they harm us, we learn, and know in our core, that *we are not safe.*

And therefore, we feel that even *God* does not truly love us or protect us.

It is so challenging for us to know, to understand—in the inaccessible unconscious—that our story of what our parent *is to us* and apparently *feels about us* is simply *not the total truth of us.*

Now, I see that my father is the *Light of Spirit in Reality*. I perceive him as "run" by impersonal conditioned programs and wounds that blocked the expression of that *Light*. As humans we all share this common bond of vulnerability to being overtaken by these life-negating volatile, mental-emotional survival fears.

Programs and patterns consist of thoughts, beliefs, reactions, and emotions. For example, a pattern of low self-worth leads to habitually invalidating others. An internal program of feeling humiliated leads to forcefully resisting disrespect. A personality often simply consists of an accumulation of these unexamined patterns.

Tremendous power arises in examining these patterns, and inquiring as to the true, authentic self beneath and beyond them.

The sense of a personal "me"—as separate from the Divine— is run by these limiting or wounding programs, until the *Light of Reality* as *Spirit* dawns.

Now, I no longer experience myself as a helpless victim. I experienced *"the"* pain of *"the"* unconsciousness, seeming to operate as a person in the form of my father. This is what occurs, en masse, when we feel separate from *God, from Divine Grace*.

We fell into this collective misidentification "together," and we awaken "together". In candid intelligence we commit to the inner path to the *Sacred Self*.

Now, rather than the invasive dirge of "shame is," "unworthiness is," the celestial symphony sings on: *God Is, Light Is*.

Identity has shifted from knowing "self" as a girl or woman— with a past, a persona, and programs—to more and more deeply knowing *Self as Spirit*.

Though pain from the traumas still arises at times, the pain does not debilitate or freeze me. My heart breaks open—moment by moment—to feel the highest heights of true love, to express the deepest depths of compassion's ocean.

There is crystal clear knowing of being *one with the Ultimate Father, God Presence.*

Adoration *Is*, adoration lives the life.

Devotion fulfills the heart and reveals it as still *Home* in the innocence, sacredness and beauty of Original Creation.

The pain remains as a lingering remembrance—not personal, yet *known*—in a way that all living beings are seen, in some deep place, as *Sacred*. The memory of our own pain imbues us with compassion for every suffering heart who appears in front of our face. Being treated as less than sacred is the core root emotional cancer of the humans.

This pain awakens a deep passion for *Sacredness Accepted, as the relevant, practical ground of being.* In this way we come *Home* to *Sacredness*, and we say "Yes, *I am That.*"

Sacredness Accepted, as the *real*, is the eternal, pervading and permanent answer to: the freeze. The realization *I Exist as Spirit, One with God*, is the answer that goes deep enough to truly heal all trauma and pain.

And all that God Is—whether we think of it as Creator, as Light, as Holy Spirit—is pure, indescribable Love.

That love is akin to devotion, trust, adoration.

It is a pure, sweet, inexpressibly deep, unfathomably strong Love.

In that *Eternal Love* an indescribable safety arises, and rests. And in that *Love is Oneness*.

Father Ahavah!

Father — our oneness with God Presence, our Eternal Spirit Self.

And *Ahavah* - the everlasting, unconditional, immensity of *Divine Love*. (Ahavah means love in the Hebrew language).

Alive as Father Ahavah, I Exist as That!

Experiential Application:

The Presence Only Love Is,

Dissolving Trauma Memories,

Restoring Calm Presence

Remember that truth is simple. The following phrases are not intended as complex steps or formulas. Rest from trying to learn or achieve. Release concepts of pass or fail.

Simply read each sentence and relax into it.

Close your eyes and rest in the message between every phrase or two, and reopen your eyes to read more.

The following experiential messages support the healing of trauma. They heal by revealing that *the presence of Peace* is *always within*.

Take your time. Receive the experiential contemplations as a gift to savor. Open to a supportive, comforting and illuminating remembrance of *Oneness with Father Ahavah, Eternal Creator*.

The experiential applications in this book welcome a coming *Home*.

Father Ahavah

Father Ahavah Contemplative Prayer

- Rest and relax into a comfortable position
- Breathe in a circular breath, without pausing on the top of the inhale or the bottom of the exhale
- Continue with this slow, deep, circular breath, while allowing the body to relax into soft ease
- One by one, relax the eyes... face... jaw... shoulders...
- Have awareness of being safe, and loved in this moment, no matter what is happening in a current life situation or what has happened at any time in life
- Have awareness of anything in the life span that felt like a blow, that led to a freeze
- It may have been physical, relational, emotional, medical, financial—anything
- Allow one incident to arise
- See this as memory... symbolic of patterns
- See the memory and patterns as fluid and changeable—as similar to last night's dream—the same mental-emotional constitution of a dream
- Have awareness of any belief or thought around the memory
- Have awareness that beliefs encase and thus trap the feelings—making them less volatile or strong—yet preventing their release and resolution
- When we move from the space of heart feeling to the box of mental thinking, the feeling gets trapped as inaccessible

- ...cted by thoughts, story, or commentary — ...e the feeling
- ...ughts, beliefs, emotions to flow like a stream or ...ng into background
- Just as you do not need to know where a river comes from for it to flow unnoticed, you do not need to know where thoughts or emotions come from
- Simply be with the emotional sensations arising in this moment, open, soft… let go… relax more
- Now shift from the more surface thought-emotion to the deeper *Spirit Presence* within
- *Contemplate: "I Am Sacred, One with Eternal Changeless Love"*
- *This Eternal Love Presence is always here… open to feel this*
- Be the *Sacredness Accepted, more real than suffering,* and see pain less personal "to you"
- Allow it to be *"the pain"*, rather than "my personal pain"
- *Sacredness Accepted* welcomes the sensations/emotions into *Love*
- The neurological system calms, and resets to this *Safe Holiness Love*
- Feel and release the numbness of any prior freeze
- Open the heart to trustworthy *Father Ahavah Love*
- Open the heart even more and rest in: *"I exist as Divinity, Spirit Presence"*
- Feel that as more *Real* than any trauma, hurt, or stress
- Allow the trauma-body or stress-body to remember that the inner *Peace* is more *Real* than the anxiety or stress — this is a huge key — take a moment to feel this

- The place in you that has memories of the past—the history body—now opens to *Divine Love*... as if it has only ever known gentleness, kindness, respect, peace
- Rest deeper in the heart, and allow the bodily tension to unwind and soften
- Open to feel *Spirit Presence, the Eternal Light,* as total Love... *with no absence of Love*
- Quietly contemplate that, and "fall back" into that
- No longer identifying with the body and emotions as the primary identity— see this as a significant key
- Realize: *I Am Spirit, and only Love ever happened in Spirit*
- Allow the *Eternal Spirit Love,* to be felt as the most real *Presence* of you
- Open to view the *Eternal God Light* as the truest reality of the physicality, even if it doesn't seem so... rest in this
- Release the general weight of memories and history, to feel the light, bright *Aliveness as Sacredness Accepted*

The Hebrew spelling of Ahavah (Love)

Selah!

Chapter Two

The Swallow

From The Swallowing Truth To Being Heard as The Divine Voice

Then

Shopping.

But not for me.

I tagged along with my father and his girlfriend. I had little hope of ever being the main show, other than the day I won cheerleading princess. Each year of childhood I felt like more like a tag along and a burden.

We strolled around Countryside Mall, a place to go when life is so boring you will put up with the plastic feel and humdrum offerings just for something to do. It felt like a waste of a day.

I wondered exactly why I went shopping with Dad and his girlfriend. Clearly ten-year-old me was not authentically part of the "two of them." No golden threads of affinity lit up between them and me.

I quietly observed the distancing dance of their blaming sparks grow hotter. I heard the clashing tones of their words deteriorate into discord. My stomach tightened into a rubber ball, in an unsuccessful attempt to control the vulnerable anxiety swirling inside.

His disinterested shrugs grew more flippant; her eyes flashed more disgust. She emanated the understandable resentment of a young woman longing for affection, while powerless to receive it. I felt compassion.

By now, I was so miserable and fatigued from the tension, that I just wanted to go home. I missed my mother… maybe. I wasn't sure. I *lost her* in the divorce. Battling with her depression, my mom couldn't focus on me anymore. Her house failed to offer me the secure solace of nurturing warmth.

But somehow, being around my father and his girlfriend made me miss her. I felt alone, out of place everywhere. I wished I had *somewhere to go,* somewhere to hide.

In Nicole's fashion store, she finally gave up trying to find something that would light him up. He missed the intensity of the moment. So she resorted to a subtle rebellion to stand up for herself and bolster her self-respect. We were leaving.

I marched out the door of the mall, in the lead. I couldn't wait to get home and walk out in the clean open ocean air, away from the suffocating dissatisfaction.

As I turned to see if they were coming, Dad's girlfriend said, "I didn't find anything; I am not going to the party tonight."

What happened next imprinted a message so clear, so sharp, so all-pervasive that it affected my relationship with every man I encountered from then on, through my young womanhood.

The father I longed to respect, trust, and feel safe with, suddenly spiraled into a storm of cynical scorn. His double punch landed squarely on her nose and top lip, splitting them into flowing red rivers of blood.

He angrily spewed out, with immense hatred, "That is what my ex used to do and that is why she is my ex. When we get home, pack your shit and get out."

I cringed as I witnessed this violent intolerance for the feminine expression. It silenced my self-expression, stripping the *power to "be heard"* from my voice. It choked off the feminine within me and spiked my neurological system. I felt an aching, rising grief.

Mom was now *"the ex."* And in that moment, it was clear that *he* had left *her*, and that it was because she *pulled stuff*.

If you pull stuff or make someone unhappy you get violently beaten or abandoned.

Out of the corner of my eye, I detected wild movements as a blond-haired woman in the parking lot screamed and tried to restrain her husband from attacking my father.

My heart pounded in my ears, as I caught my breath in this surreal moment. I felt nausea and shock. So many levels of psychological, emotional, and bodily suffering occurred in such a compressed space of time.

I trembled in shame as an invisible weight descended upon me. I involuntarily crouched like some unseen force cloaked my shoulders with a dark lead coat—and then sauntered off—leaving me to bear too heavy of a burden for a little girl to lift off alone.

The weight sat directly on top of my shoulders, and pressed down, hard. By the time of this event I had cried many tears from the times trauma stole my childhood play, joy and innocence. Yet this time, the tears froze inside, like tributaries turned to crystal, unable to flow. I rigidly mustered my composure. Like a wooden statue, I stared straight ahead.

Dad's pickup truck had a bench seat, so we all sat in the front cab.

There we sat side by side... all three of us lined up.

We drove down the road, six eyes looking straight ahead, no one daring to look at the other... not even stealing a glance out of the corner of the eye.

Like three stone weights, feeling trauma's cold sting...

Don't look, don't feel, don't speak.

Don't look within. Keep staring straight ahead.

Don't look inside. Keep looking out there.

My father drove, eyes staring straight ahead. His girlfriend dabbed away at her bleeding face, sitting next to him. I pressed my body up against the truck door, half hoping it would open and I would fall out.

Then Dad chirped, "Ann Marie, it looks like there is a new ice cream store being built there up ahead." That instant sparked an immense swirling confusion. How could he speak as if nothing had happened?

He wasn't saying, "My God, I am sorry, please forgive me. We all have to love each other and be kind." He wasn't saying, "Ann Marie, I made a mistake, and it's serious and I'll correct it and women shouldn't be hit." He wasn't saying, "I don't want this to affect our relationship. I love you, and I want to repair this and for us to be close." He wasn't saying "Ann Marie, this won't happen again in our family; we will care for each other." He wasn't saying, "I don't really hate your Mom and it wasn't all her fault. Women are to be loved and cherished." He wasn't saying, "I am in pain and overwhelmed. I feel hurt by women and life, and I do not want you to suffer from that".

He was saying normal, everyday things.

I longed to speak from the depths of my pain, but the words died in my throat. By then, there had been so many traumas, losses, and rejections. I longed to say: *Look at what you are doing! You've already hurt my body physically in the past, and my mom too, and ruined my love for you! You can't do this to us!*

I ached to say: *I am leaving. I am moving out. I want to be away from you! I have no parents!"* I secretly wished to open the walls around my heart, and quietly implore: *I love you; why do you sometimes hate me? I so much wish to be close to you, and for you to love me and be my Dad.*

I longed to say: *I hate the divorce! and I miss my Mom! and why is this girl only a few years older than my brother even here?* And I wanted to say, *But if she's here, how can you hit her?* I wanted to cry out: *My life is a nightmare, and I don't think anybody cares. In fact, I am totally sure no one is noticing, and I am dying inside here!*

But most of all I just wanted to cry, and to be a daughter child, and to say, *Please be my Daddy.*

I wanted a Dad so badly.

A father.

At this most critical moment, I choked.

Could not speak.

Could not speak up.

I had seen too much of his anger; I learned my voice and words lacked value. I feared non-compliance. I had learned I was the burden, and had yet to discover my inner courage to speak the truth to the men close to my heart.

I knew there was a God, a Creator, that *just had* to be Love. No one taught me, but I sat and prayed for long periods of time. And these prayers were deep love communions with/as God Presence. Much older, I discovered that most children never experienced these rare, deep spiritual communions.

Yet, the pain of my little world still felt more real than the immense stunning *Reality of God's Light*. Being spiritually *Home*, had not yet anchored as the ground of being. I had not yet commanded the depth of *Presence* to call "another being" *Home*.

So… I stared straight ahead and surrendered up some monotone answer.

The swallow.

I swallowed the intensity of the rising emotions and the cries of my heart.

It felt so icky to answer. I sat there, backed into a conflicted corner with no way to win. I felt like I still had to love him, to be loyal to him, and not shame him.

I had learned that his feelings mattered more than my own.

He stopped the car. My heart started to pound again. I sat there, nervous and shaky. As he slammed the car door shut, I realized he was just going into a convenience store to pick something up. That landed me in an awkward predicament.

I felt extremely uncomfortable and vulnerable. *Please God, don't let her say anything to me.* I stared straight ahead.

Of course, she said something to me.

Of course, she asked the worst questions.

"Did he do this to your Mom? What's wrong with him? Is this how you guys are?"

I noticed that since he struck her, she hadn't spoken to him, only to me. And I noticed he was only speaking to me, not to her. Usually they ignored me and spoke to each other. Now they avoided speaking to each other and spoke through me.

The Mom comment he made in the parking lot really stung—I could feel how much he hated her. I thought he hated me too.

He hated our *feminine*.

I felt a deep sadness. It was hard to tell if the grief arose more from him *hating our feminine*, or hating my mom. I finally surmised it hurt more that he hated Mom.

Later, I sat outside of our house, pondering in confusion and shaking. I waited for her to come out with her suitcases, packed and leaving. She never came out. She never left him.

I couldn't digest what had happened. *He* hit her, but *she* was to blame. *She* would be put on the street: "Pack your shit and get out," he'd said. But then he did nothing about that.

I didn't understand why she didn't leave. Nobody left.

At least not for a while, until the day came I was told to leave.

No one ever said a word to me about the day he hit her. Nothing was ever addressed, nothing was healed, nothing was ever done.

The pattern continued… without reparation… until the next time.

No one ever asked how I felt or comforted me. My neurological system hiked up more, and grief hung like a heavy, wet, foggy insulation around my heart.

Alone.

Lost.

And I missed my Mom.

Now

In many ways, looking back is like watching a movie of someone else's life. I'm not dissociating—there is no suppression or break from reality.

Rather, I have clear remembrance of the precise emotions and thoughts that arose as the early life events occurred. I re-experience the tight stomach, the "oh no" horrified feeling, the nauseous resistance to what occurred.

Yet, I no longer experience the events as the prior identity would... as the little girl, or as a personality identifying as this "Ann" character. This happened to a person that I *know*, and though I can feel her bodily sensations, I no longer live from *that identity*. *I Am Spirit* arises as the more true, more tangible reality than any emotions, thoughts or sensations of the character.

I exist as *Spirit Presence*, and that seems to express through the body-mind of Ann. Yet, it's more seamless than "express through."

I now wonder if it would have been better to speak and risk being hit, than to shut down my honest expression of the call for sanity.

I could have opened my heart, moved through the fear, and spoken directly—regardless of consequences. I wished to voice the call to integrity and the appeal to love that passionately burned in my heart, as a summoning *Home to Love*.

Yet, I didn't know identity as *Spirit Presence*—not in a tangible way in these shocking moments of trauma. I had yet to establish roots as *Presence, heart wings of true Home* in the midst of the chaos of this world. I couldn't call my father *Home* if I still lived in the proverbial Kansas.

Now, I am able to observe a prior mass of trauma, like a tightly woven ball of spaghetti, and discern and untangle every strand. I give voice and language to its vibrational qualities, its perceptual consequences. For example, when I see the image of my father hitting his partner, I feel my throat tighten with a strong message to not express my true feelings. I see the image of her shocked face, and I feel the vibration of a woman's defeat and worthlessness. I experience the deep smoldering sense of being imprinted as inferior to men, existing only to make them happy or bring them pleasure.

Looking back, I see all else that I began to believe:

Neurological imprints of trauma (twenty times more impactful than imprints of more calm and happy times) created a belief that relationships are not safe or stable. The objectification of the feminine obscured the belief in sacredness. The neutral or "good" times with my father: when he took me water skiing, or we made chocolate chip cookies, or when he was friendly toward me, did not compensate for the trespasses.

The times of connection seemed hollow, trivial and surface-level compared to the deeper lack of protection and gross insensitivity and abuse. The "normal" times did not balance, compensate for, or erase, the depth and frequencies of the rejections, neglects and traumas.

Over the years, the imprints of abuse and pain—embraced in the potency and immensity of *Spirit Light*—have faded and lost power.

This marks the pathway out of the pain.

Now, rather than believing that I am a victim of an abusive father, I see that at the core identity, I am that which is far beyond a body-mind, personal "me" Ann. Rather I exist as *Spirit*, immersed in and as the reality of *God Presence*. And in that *Presence*, that *Aliveness, Immense Love is!*

I can trace Ann's journey—through profound suffering—to an unwinding of neurological imprints, beliefs, thoughts, and emotions of her prior self. This divine undoing reveals deeper imprints of the energetic content of: disrespected, dishonored, disempowered, not heard.

Past events seem more impersonal to an "Ann" character who is not the whole of "me." I realize that my earthly dad, in ultimate reality, is the same Spirit *Presence* that *I feel* each day. That *Spirit Light*, that unifying vital force of "self", of "other" stands as most real.

His imprinting, akin to global patterning, influenced him to deal with his wounds and fears by erupting in rage. He learned those conditioned feelings and reactions. Yet his "real self" exists as Spirit, one with God Presence.

We embrace the higher pathways, by moving beyond personal victims. Mistreatment and cruelty is a "virus" of our collective unconscious, due to forgetting our true nature. Who is our Creator and what are we created as, in reality? Do we intimately know the Eternal Light? Or have we forgotten?

It's a paradox. On one hand, no one is personally responsible; we are all here to remember *Eternal Presence*. We remember in this context, of such misalignment of reverence and love. On the other hand, each being sits completely responsible—able to respond—to remember *Home* and release all that anesthetizes the heart.

We stand accountable when we allow covert passive-aggressive patterns or overt violence to take over— and we do nothing to directly look at and address those shadows—to remember our *True Life*.

In a sense, there is nothing "out there" but our sum-total thinking-ness, our believing-ness, our feeling-ness. The landscape of our lives beautifies, as we immerse in the *real*. Then childhood is a memory, made of the same stuff as last night's dream. And the "dreams" of today hit a zenith over the rainbow, to a pure land, refined and kind.

Then we feel *Reality*, beyond all images, scenes, life dramas. And we know of that *Golden Reality: I Am That*.

The liberation from autumn's mists of doubt, and winter's chill of loss, arises in feeling the satisfying warmth of Light happening on the inside. Know *that as more real* than what we perceive with five physical senses. It's a whole shift of identity. Nothing else fulfills the inner incompletion that drives all worrying, wanting and wondering.

When we identify as a psychological "me," when the limited historical "person" is the axis around which identity spins, then small kindnesses or little triumphs cannot gloss over the lack of sacredness.

No amount of success, whether in relationships, college degrees, six-figure incomes, masterful work expressions, beautiful homes, or social sentiment—touches the wounds from sacredness shattered, or fulfills the longing for *Oneness with God Presence*.

The only lasting salve and balm, the only permanent freedom, lies within the direct face to face surrender into our ineffable *Origin*.

Liberation from the limited "me" is the deep experience of primordial tenderness and changeless compassion—*happening on the inside*—not sought on the outside. And then "inside" and "outside" mirror simple exquisite synergy.

The eternal relationships, that reside deeper than human sentiment or changing "love", exist as *sacred* at their core essence. True relationships light the world with the recognition of the *Light* between the *two* that makes *not two*.

The truest love is the love for, and as, *Divine Presence, and the Divine* within all beings —not the sentimental attachments to objects and physical persons. As we experience identity *as Spiritual Love*, it sensitizes us to what we contemplate, pray, and express.

One day out in nature, breathing in rhythm with flowing waters, feeling the wind on my face and hearing it rustle the leaves of the soaring trees... deep reverence dawned in the *trustworthiness* of *Father Ahavah, God Presence*. I heard: *above all else... trust this...* **trust this.**

The "unconditioned way" of **being** awakens in gentle glory... the unlearned way of *Being Love*.

We look with humility, courage, and stark honesty into the patterns of the "learned way"... learned in order to survive... and we firmly set them down, and softly let them go.

Life constantly invites us to look at the shadows, the fears, the blindspots, the "me" conditioning. We are called to look at the shadows cast by traumas—to feel the darkness, and spontaneously surrender to the power of the *Divine Love* that dissolves them into thin air.

The suffering does not have ultimate power. It only seems to have power when we deny it ... ignore it... and say things like, "Look over there at the ice cream store." When we truly, deeply see the consequence of humankind's trespasses—the threat of extinction, the rivers of tears, the hearts sweating blood, then we have to stop.

We stop.

And we see that humanity's inward and outward pool of unsolved problems—of cutting trespass—lives on year-in and year-out... lifetime in and lifetime out... millennia in and millennia out.

And we passionately call for an answer.

The true answer.

The permanent liberation.

And then we don't swallow the avalanche of trivia—from the barrage of public media to the gossip of coffee shop chats—threatening to dilute us. And then we don't have the heart to escape from the pain of existential separation from God Presence, and pretend the ice cream store up ahead will hide it.

Experiential Application

I Am the Voice That Remembers Home

Born of Divinity

Remember that truth is simple. These are not complicated steps to learn, memorize or acquire.

There is no need to try, get it right, or perform. Simply relax, and open to an immersion of peace and grace.

Read each phrase or two and close eyes and relax into the essence of the phrase. You don't have to think too much about it or analyze it.

Allow the essence of the message to engender the direct experience of peace, and the restoration of remembrance of *Oneness with God Presence, Eternal Love.*

Father Ahavah Contemplation

- Relax into a comfortable position
- Breathe slowly, deeply, fully
- Place awareness around the eyes

- Allow the little muscles around the eyes to relax and go soft
- Release the tension around anything you ever saw you did not wish to see
- You do not have to think of any certain memories or incidents... have a general intention... allow emotions to be free of stories or events
- If memories arise, let go of attention to persons or situations, and place awareness on the story-free emotional sensation
- Simply have a soft intention to release any resistance to anything you saw
- Place awareness on your left ear
- Release contraction, tension, around anything you heard that you did not wish to hear or anything you wished you heard but did not hear
- Have an awareness of peace as you place awareness on your left ear
- Repeat the above three steps for the right ear
- Have awareness of any sensation of "swallowing" "your truth"
- Release tension from the throat, neck, jaw
- Have awareness of any sense of weight, worry, burden, upon your shoulders
- Allow your shoulders to go soft
- Breathe in deeply into the lungs and release any residue of grief
- Release any tightness in the abdomen... torso... hips

- Relax the whole body... slowly scan the body and allow a deep restfulness
- Consciously release any numbness to feelings of trespass—from trauma
- Have an intention for anesthetized feelings to have permission to surface gently, welcomed and released with ease... take a moment for this
- Open for the softness of Divine Love, happening within, to soften and immerse grievances in the space of unconditional love
- Allow the tension, contracted emotional pain, to open and soften... to flow and fade in the ocean of *Peace, of Spirit Presence*, that is *You*
- *Take a moment for this...*
- *Rest in "I am safe in this moment"*
- Imagine that anxiety, fight or flight, neurological sense of threat, calms at a profound level
- Realize: *"I exist as Spirit, Peace Presence"*... take a moment to close your eyes and rest in this
- Feel this *Peace* permeate your whole being, neurological system, thoughts, feelings... really *deeply respond to the reality of peace... trust this*
- See thoughts as clouds passing by, as objects coming for your attention... that no longer receive your attention... rest in the heart peace
- Have greater interest in inner freedom, than in the chattering thoughts of the mind
- Create a safe space for any un-cried tears to surface and flow

- Have awareness of buried feelings of being disappointed or crushed… feel and release
- Feel any arising longing for respect, for kindness… release the sensation of longing…
- Contemplate speaking from the heart and being heard: "*I speak, I am heard when it matters most*"… rest in this…
- *Softly Be Home…* contemplating: "*I Am the voice that remembers Eternal Home… here, now*
- As deeply as you can, feel heard by *God, Spirit, The Eternal*
- Open to the warmth of *Paternal Protective Love*
- Merge with this cherishing love… this affirming and strengthening *Love*
- Open to *Father Ahavah! (Everlasting, Unconditional Father God Love)*
- Rest deeply as *Heard*
- Feel: *I Am the Spirit Voice*
- *I am heard by Father Ahavah! Yet,* One with *Father Ahavah* like the ocean hears and is one with its wave…
- Feel so safe, there is no opposite to this safe
- Heard by, One with *Father Ahavah*…

Selah!

Chapter Three

The Wall:

From the Wall
To Heaven's Immortal Wings

Then

At the age of nine, I still lived with Mom in the black and white house on Fairmont Street. By the time I was eleven, I had moved five more times.

Growing up turned into a lot of moving, moving, moving.

To face life meant facing perpetual uprooting—of home, of bonds, of ties, of nurture, of family, of commitment, of security… of virtually every single thing that meant anything.

Uprooted.

Again.

I was staying with my Dad and his girlfriend for at least the summer, or possibly permanently.

I was the daughter.

Or at least I *had imagined* I was the daughter.

A guest visited for two weeks—a relative of my father's girlfriend. She was the same age as my older brother. I wished my brother were there instead. The guest constantly picked at me, made fun of me.

I cringed at her unkind inflections, snotty voice, and cutting ways. How did she drop down into the middle of my little world? In the smog of these tensions, the small house felt like a suffocating cellar. This guest felt like a wall of resistance.

She just thrived on bullying and competition. One of her tricks involved sneaking into the bathroom, locking the door, and exiting through the back bathroom door, to tan in the back yard. When I asked her why she made the only bathroom unusable to me for hours on end, she laughed with great satisfaction that she "beat me" at tanning. I didn't know we were having a contest. I remember her smug delight every time she bullied and beat me at some competition that I didn't even know existed.

One day I sat by the ocean alone, crying. And then I thought of the medals I won at my elementary school's field day contest. I didn't try to beat anyone or make them feel inferior. I just did my best. No one made fun of anyone, or taunted them, or called them names.

Rather than compete with her, I withdrew.

But one day, this bullying guest defeated me in a way that broke my heart and shattered the core of my self-esteem. Not only was *I* unaware of being in a contest with her for my father's love, *she* probably wasn't either. But she "won" anyway.

Dad and his girlfriend took late afternoon naps.

My brother wasn't around. *He was never around for the really bad moments.*

The guest was yelling at me… again. This usually happened when no one was home. As she was older and bigger than me, I usually retreated to the outside to get away from her.

This day sheets of rain poured down, so I stayed inside and kept quiet. Until I hit a breaking point and then I talked back. She yelled louder.

Suddenly the door to Dad's room jerked open. He stormed out and without asking what was happening, immediately told *me* to pack all of my "shit."

He told his ten year old daughter to pack and to leave, severing the foundation of the father daughter relationship.

He allowed the guest, who bullied and instigated, to stay.

The daughter was the guest and the guest was the daughter.

Really, the daughter was *nothing and no one.*

The one who was more kind, sensitive, caring was the least protected, nurtured, loved.

Again, the world turned upside down and *there was no order.*

Everything was always out of order and twisted around.

Out of order.

My ears heard, from my Father, "I...was...to... pack...all...of... my... shit."

But what mattered was what my heart heard.

My heart heard the expression on his face, the tone of his voice, the rejecting energy, which drove my shaky childlike esteem into the bare ground.

My heart heard messages that I might never recover from.

I heard: *You are not my daughter.*

I heard: *I do not want you.*

I heard: *You are not my priority*

I heard: *I do not love and protect you; I join with those who are against you.*

What I heard was: you are a burden, a part of me wishes you didn't exist.

I wished I didn't exist.

A deep humiliation seeped into my bones.

By then, when rejection occurred... *again*... everything—my body, thoughts, and emotions—trembled with shock and confusion.

I felt the primal agonies of a sensitive, creative, mystical creature. One so sensitive can respond to the guidance as light as a feather, or as fluid as a gentle flowing stream. Instead, I was stunned by a tidal wave of sharp cruelty.

The wall won.

The unyielding wall streamrolls over kindness, caring or balance. It smothers wonder, enchantment, and the spontaneous joy of kindled camaraderie.

The unremitting wall oppresses the natural magical impulse to bond, share and give. The wall of dominance and indifference stops the rhythm of love, like a sharp rock thrown into the spokes of a turning wheel ends all forward progress.

It sabotages love.

The wall sabotages the miracle of connection, communion and trust.

When the wall wins, everyone loses. When the wall crumbles, love wins.

In those days, love wasn't winning.

When love loses, the voice of love is not heard.

The voice, crouching behind the wall, falters breathlessly. It has no authority, no lung-power, no impetus of expression. It has no right to its words, its message or its heart impulses. It has no birthright to exist.

Self-sovereignty is lost.

I didn't know what to do with the wall.

Life became *a problem*.

Other kids colored; I scaled the wall.

I perceived that other families communicated, formed bonds, made craft books of warm memories; I hid in the shadow of the wall, and stared at the movie screen of my aloneness.

My psyche, spun into confusion, couldn't make meaning out of the chaos.

My sense of esteem plummeted.

As repetitive demoralizing experiences occurred, life lost meaning. Faced with distorted paradigms of love, I scrambled to find vital belonging or reason to exist here. I grappled to dig up some relevant meaning in the meaningless.

Anyway... then, all my stuff was packed.

There we sat again, in the pick-up truck, staring straight ahead.

Driving down the road, staring straight ahead.

I swallowed back the tears, and sat numbly obedient, afraid to speak what I knew and felt.

We pulled up to the black and white house on Fairmont Street. He dropped me off, pulled out of the driveway, and I imagined, drove back to *his* home, staring straight ahead.

I thought, "I guess I'm living with Mom now!?" I walked into my old bedroom and the pink gingham bedspread was gone. The bed was gone. My bedroom was gone.

I sat alone in the little house.

Unable to dam up the tears another second, I crouched there in my long pigtails and cried.

Those honey-brown pigtails had gained popularity at grade school. One day, so many boys pulled my pigtails at recess that I marched into the principal's office, unannounced. He looked up in great surprise; students did not usually barge into his office.

At school, having a voice must have felt safe. I had the courage to clearly convey to the highest authority in the school that these were *my pigtails*, and under no circumstances did I want them *pulled*.

Years later I realized all the boys pulled my pigtails because they thought I was cute.

I didn't have time for, didn't care about, cute. I ached to be wanted. I wanted a real family. I wanted a father who loved me. I didn't have time for kid's stuff.

I had lived in that room with the pink gingham when my parents were married. It was the refuge I ran to, where I peeked out from a crack in my door as the fights grew larger and the love got smaller. It was the house where the family died a little more every day, until only loneliness lived there.

When I did cry, there were so many buried tears that it seemed they'd never stop. But I was not comforted. It was like a valve released some pressure, yet the pain did not stop. Sadness quietly sat, and stayed—deep in the heart, in the lungs, in the throat, in the eyes, in the head.

I couldn't get away from the layers of veiled sadness. Sadness was as familiar as my hands and feet. I felt it all around me and inside me so poignantly that I could detect it anywhere it lingered, no matter how people tried to mask it.

The man who just lost his job, laughing too loudly at a party—I could feel the sadness there. And the well-known couple, who had only a superficial connection, posing with their plastic smiles for a camera; I felt their hollow bleakness. Again and again, time would reveal the accuracy of my "sadness meter." I could feel the condensation of compressed sorrow in those around me, like a metal detector picks up the frequencies of lost coins.

The night got later, and sometime past eleven I decided I'd better figure out dinner. I ate cold spinach out of a can, thinking it would give me strength.

Sometime after midnight the front door opened. I was lying on a sheet on the living room floor, with a towel over me.

Mom was not alone. Some strange man with black curly hair was with her.

I will never forget the look on her face. Her expression went from laughing and talking happily to completely disgusted.

Then came the next chilling slap in my long day of serial icy barbs.

She said irritably, "What are you doing here?" That was followed by a discordant, "I do not want you here now!" Her disappointment could not be more evident. I was a burden to her.

She did not speak like a mother to her loved child: *"Honey, what are you doing here? How lovely, I missed you."* Nor with: *"Are you ok? what happened?"*

Her words spewed out like a shaken fermented drink, foaming up and spilling out all over a pristine carpet.

The pain bubbled up like I had been kicked in the stomach. It went up through the chest, the throat, and on up until it pressed against my head and scalp. It felt like some awful thing was trying to get out, but it just couldn't. I wished it would just pour out and flow over and stain the carpet, like my mother's words. Instead it just seemed to stain me inside with an unrelenting shame.

I wished I didn't exist.

Why did I have to exist?

Why was I even alive?

I had been completely rejected *as a daughter.* I was not part of a family. I didn't seem to matter to anyone. This worthlessness, this gnawing doubt as to my value, ever generated an aching emptiness.

These thoughts and feelings grew and grew over the years. When I was fourteen, I began to think of ways to "not be here." Late in my teens, I attempted to end my existence.

There was no foundation, no sacred edifice, or temple of true purpose. There were only endless walls that said "no" to open innocence.

I lay there through the night, hot tears flowing down my cheeks. My life felt so heavy, so empty.

I distinctly remember thinking of trying to die. Then something happened, and I could feel God; I could feel the *Divine Presence.*

Not think of God, but FEEL God.

These angelic remembrances occurred unsought, spontaneously, and at strange and unexpected times.

Once, as a very young child, I saw a cockroach on the front steps, dying. A little tear of compassion welled up. And then I *felt God.* I felt Spirit in or around the cockroach, and that Spirit was alive. And I could also feel that Spirit in my body. And I could feel it in my cat, and my doggie.

It came at certain moments; ordinary time seemed to stop, and I profoundly experienced some clearer, higher *Reality*. *And in this Reality of God Presence, happening in the heart, all was Light, all was Love, all was glorious, all was in order. And there was a warm, peaceful knowing, and a sense of great wisdom in awareness of our Creator.*

When I sneaked off alone by the sea, I felt that I was Spirit—vast and free—spreading out over the ocean and reaching up to the sky. And that Spirit did not feel this agony and pain. I felt a *Golden Presence*, like a *Mother-Father Spirit*, that was my true and only parent.

However, those moments were rare. And I felt the wall pressing the knowingness out of me... forcing my attention on survival. The mounting, painful feelings and emotions cascaded more often.

I felt trapped on some planet where people forgot how to love, and forgot about God. I said to myself, *There is no real love here in this place.* Yet, simultaneously, I remembered a time, and a *Presence of pure Light,* that touched my heart with a breathtaking feeling of *Home*. It glimmered like a diamond-light kingdom formed of silvery gold luminous love and light, before all time... *when all was kind*. I felt glimpses... like a vague knowing... of the *Origin*... but then I just couldn't... remember.

The amnesia took over again and I huddled in tight—a little girl in a little body in a big world that felt very scary... and a big wall that felt wildly and wickedly unyielding.

Now

Reality is more real than the wall.

Those rare moments of "then," when I knew myself as *Spirit Presence,* now exist as the pervading Reality.

The wall is not seen as something outside, like a person, place, thing, or event.

The wall is not seen as a force to fight against or avoid.

The wall has to be walked through.

We cannot fight our belief in our insignificance, or battle the suspicion of our irrelevance. We cannot jump over the walls of our resisted feelings. We cannot dig holes under the walls of stubborn persons who wish to keep the status quo—no matter how insane or unsustainable that defended status quo appears.

The wall has to be walked through.

We do this by being *Light* and by seeing the wall as *Light.*

This means identifying, through deep contemplation and realization, "I Am Spirit." And it means de-solidifying the outer walls of rejection, cruelty, competition, greed, unsustainability, denial, and insensitivity.

This deconstruction of the wall happens by descaling the calcified layers of experiences, allowing fluidity to the rigid stored emotions, nullifying agreement with conditioned beliefs.

We walk through the wall by living as one with *God Presence*.

We open to that Presence and behold *It* express as the primordial voice of the symphonies of *Home as Spirit*. This voice emanates as a silent orchestra of compassion, felt and "heard" whether we verbally speak or not.

We rest in the beauty of holiness.

And we invoke the power of sanity, order, and reverence.

Finding our voice means commanding to life our Immortal Lungs, the breath and aliveness behind our voice.

Then our voice comes from our entire *Presence*, it never has to strain to be heard, or spiral into despair over being ignored out of existence. Our voice simply *Is*, because our primordial lungs *Are*.

We exist as the *Divine Breath*—the light and life of all things.

At times, when I felt blame or resentment toward my earthly parents, or deep grief and pain at their rejections, I stopped and prayed. I asked to feel their pain—that which drove their actions. I prayed to release blame and to embrace compassion.

Once when I did this, many years ago, I felt my dad's pain like a smoldering fire of deep disappointment, and my mom's pain as a profound worthlessness. I saw where his enraged disappointment merged with, and married, her despairing worthlessness. My childhood crucible birthed from that union.

When I felt their pain and released those sensations, it felt like they too were spontaneously, invisibly freed from the pain. This impersonalized it as "the pain". Then I, as daughter, was not the disappointment—though I had believed I was. I was not the worthless one—though I had believed I was. As the stored emotions released, the walls crumbled.

I felt tender compassion for my parents and what they had endured in their lives.

Facing the wall of unconsciousness turned into a spiritual initiation. When rejection came frequently and fiercely like lions in a darkened den, I again felt vulnerable, constricting my vocal cords, suppressing my lungs.

And in those times I remembered the *Heart*. And at home in the heart of God's Love, that breath filled my lungs and thundered as my voice that turned away the lions, and turned the den of suffering into a paradise of Light.

I stopped fearing the smoke and mirrors of the wall when I identified as the *Fire* of the *Light*. This *Fire* became the known point of identity.

You don't fear the smoke, when you *know* you are the *Fire*.

I rest as that voice of *Source*—the voice that always prevails.

I feel the nurturing embrace of the *Primordial Papa*, the adoring *Ahavah Father*. And yet there is no "person" resting as that or becoming one with that; there is only *That. Father Ahavah!* That *Spirit Life* Is. Alone. With no filter… no becoming… already Being.

I cannot describe the immensity of my despair, living as a girl bereft of masculine nurturing, protection, support, or love. Ultimately though, I felt the existential pain of living in a world that feels separate from the Eternal Father. This arises as the agony of intense "lack." Yet, in Spirit reality, no lack exists or is possible, or ever occurs.

And I cannot describe the ineffable tender bliss of being one with *the Divine Masculine Father…* and *the Divine Feminine Mother…* and the Light of Existence *Prior To* masculine or feminine. The sweet grace of the Divine Feminine blossoms the nectar of the heart. And being that which is prior to masculine or feminine, is completion in sublime holiness.

Though we may think of God Presence as genderless—before masculine or feminine—it may express as the essence of either or both.

These extraordinary "divine feelings" differ in quality from typical human thoughts or emotions. *Alive as Spirit,* we do not need the thoughts, commentary, emotions. Being the *All* is free, open, spacious, and direct.

No matter whether a human thought seems to be "good" or "bad," it is temporary, and false in a way, because it is in the realm of impermanence.

Whether our personal story is about me "suffering" or me "pleasuring," this "me," (ego) is simply this movement away from *Awareness-Presence,* the stillness of being. Whether it's "I don't want this" (a resistance) or "I do want that," (another form of resistance to what is happening this instant) the ego is just *a wanting* or *a not wanting*. Really simplify down to that huge key: the personal "me" ego in a perceived state of lack and separation from *Creator, is a wanting… or a not wanting*.

I want this… or I don't want that.

The egoless way is as simple as, in this spontaneous instant, Being Spirit Presence, free of wanting or not wanting. Light does not want... it Is.

Spirit is Self-Completion.

In stillness, it does not follow the "want" track, or the mind-chatter radio station. It rests as causeless peace and inner joy.

Alive as *Spirit,* we sing our song, which harmonizes with all the other celestial melodies in the angelic symphony that endlessly plays on.

I hear the silvery ospreys sing in their nest, atop the soaring pine tree, and I recognize their subtle high notes. Then I detect the crimson cardinals sing on my wooden porch, their song also perfect in its seamless rich tones. Likewise the seagull flying over the Bayou, and the ducks quacking in my pool, have their symphonic perfection. I honor this expression of heaven on earth, in acceptance and humble wonderment—not like a judge of bird songs on a field day competition.

There is no competition.

We truly cease competing when we cease fearing.

And we cease fearing when we are no longer surviving, we are *beholding*.

Humility beholds.

Arrogance—or ignorance, or mistakenness—tries, struggles, manipulates, plots, forces.

Humility opens, surrenders, trusts, and in each moment—from the most pure open space possible—responds with equanimity and acts from emptiness. It joins. It bridges the space between differences and allows peace to reign.

We were sold lies, told lies. We swallowed the lie of competition, the illusion of rejection, the nightmare of having no value, and our music died in our lungs and our song choked up in our throats.

We were shut up, shut down, by the heavy hand of the wounded masculine. It needed love so deeply, but it could only cry for love through a troubled voice of domination.

And all the while we exist as the bird singing its song, just to express its love.

All the while we exist as complete and limitless.

All the while we exist as unified in the *Divine Papa Presence,* flying free.

Already Free.

Exist as Father Ahavah, **freedom Now.**

Experiential Application:

I Speak With Immortality's Lungs

And Soft Fires of Heaven's Voice

Remember that truth is *simple*. It calls for a moment-by-moment resting as true identity. Perceive no need to learn complicated steps. Sit peacefully with each phrase and allow direct experience to dawn. Close eyes and pause often between phrases.

Father Ahavah Contemplation

- Allow the breath to be slow, deep, full
- Breathe in a circular breath, with no pause on the inhale or exhale
- Breathe more and more slowly… five or six seconds or more on the inhale and
- then on the exhale
- Relax the forehead… the jaw… the shoulders…
- Place attention on the face, softening the face, and imagine expanding the border between the skin and surrounding air so that the face expands out

- Not thinking too much about that... simply have an intention to let go of the stress, tightness, contraction around the head and face by expanding it out
- Do this also for the right side of the head... left... back
- This allows tensions to fade, stored emotions to release, and the mind to quiet
- Allow the whole body to relax, as if expanding each part of the body, one by one, to the surrounding space...
- Allow each part of the body to feel more open and light and without borders
- Have less focus and identity on the "me" body, thoughts, emotions — to feel the more subtle spiritual life
- Contemplate: *"If I exist at all — and I do — I exist as Spirit Presence, Love"*
- *Rest in this for a moment...*
- Contemplate: *"There is one power, God-Spirit-Presence-Light, and that power is kind and friendly to "me." Yet, I am one with this true Eternal Presence"*
- Have awareness of any sense of a "wall"... whether it seems internal or external, emotional or mental, financial or health-related, some pain you have experienced or some unyielding suffering
- Rather than the wall being *"my"* suffering, see it as *"the"* pain (with compassion for the collective, global suffering of feeling separate from God Presence)
- Rather than seeing the wall as powerful or unremitting, see it as temporary, changing flowing, dissolving... as if it has no momentum to continue

- See this wall as an initiation to a greater realization of *God Presence, Divine Love, the Sacred Immensity*
- See the wall as now having no other "power," no law or principle of continuation
- The wall has nothing to maintain or sustain it
- Perceive the wall as a house of cards, as a sand castle, or a cloud
- Release arising limiting or painful self-beliefs and thoughts
- Have keen awareness of any emotional storage related to the wall (failure, rejection, lack, or suffering of any kind)
- Embrace the emotions and see them merely as sensations—frozen like ice cubes—now in the warming embrace of love... softening, melting, flowing, and evaporating into nothing
- See emotions as contractions now opening... softening... fading
- Spacious fresh newness is here now
- Have awareness of—one by one—any emotional storage or contractions: in the stomach area... release... in the chest... relax... around the throat... let go... around the scalp and the head... release all tension...
- Simply focus on these areas as if releasing them to the space around you, feeling them as light as space
- Contemplate Oneness with the Creator—as a cherishing, *Divine Parent* that you are offspring of, yet fully one with and as—the same way that the ocean wave is child to the ocean, and yet one with and as vast as the ocean Contemplate: *I am one with the Divine Masculine Presence... totally cherished...*

- Feel the Eternal Presence, *of the Immortal Lungs of the Breath of God...* being the voice that speaks of simple natural glory... holiness... peace
- Not thinking about this... open to feel this... rest in this
- Be the voice, the tone, the message... of *Light*... heard as the tone of *Love*
- Allow the tone of *Light* and the orchestra of *Love to be more real this instant* than anything else
- Abide as That, Father Ahavah, the *Immortal Breath* that gives you wings...
- Feel the limitlessness of being the wings of the Divine Presence, celebrated... liberated
- Remember, *"I Am Home as That"*
- And see that *Light and Love* form as a new life of lovely happenings
- Feel *"I Am Spirit Life... One with Father Ahavah... trust in It*
- Feel this as Eternal Validity...
- Perceive past traumas as clouds, as smoke, fading into nothingness
- Feel the bright sunlight of being the Daughter of the Fire, Son of the Fire, the Fire of
- Spirit, that blazes as the gentle eternal flame of freedom
- *Abide as One with Father Ahavah, The Immortal Breath of the Eternal Fire of Life*
- *Free Forever*

אהבה

Selah!

Chapter Four

Forgotten:

From The Unconsiousness That Numbs To Self-Complete Happiness

Then

This early morning, eight years old and in my pajamas, I walked to the kitchen to make a bowl of Captain Crunch cereal. I had to pass near my parents' bedroom.

Rubbing my sleepy eyes, and trying not to trip in my oversized slippers, I heard voices growing louder and louder.

Then I heard a sharp slap, followed by silence.

I held my breath; my heart beat faster and faster.

I detected Mom's voice—shaken and reprimanding, so at least she was okay physically. Her tone seemed to say, *How could you?*

I wanted to go to my Mom, but was afraid to go to their door. By this age, I could sense my father's anger, like a concrete wall that said, *Stop. Freeze. You are going to get hurt.*

The freeze mostly happened in the head, neck and throat. It bottled up, stiff as a thin steel plate made of un-cried tears and unreturned expressions of love.

I ran back across the living room and hid in my bedroom. Cautious and stealthy, I slowly and quietly cracked the door and peeked out through it, straining my ears to hear.

My father opened the door and stomped out, and then he turned back into their room, leaving the door ajar. With determined fury, he roared, "I want a divorce." He hastily rummaged in his tall chest of drawers and yanked out a white hankie. He always carried a white hankie with him.

What did that word mean?

Divorce.

I surmised that whatever *divorce meant*, it was very, very bad. It was something you did to someone who was very naughty, someone that you wanted to cast away from you, so that they would never come back. My heart and chest sank in defeat.

Life was going to change dramatically. Up until then, despite the tension, we had at least some sense of stability, of cohesiveness, of family. We ate dinner together at the table. We visited Grandma and went to the beach and I made sand castles. Every day Dad came home from work.

Every night, I felt relieved—or *something*—when his truck pulled up, even though feelings of separation mounted. I sometimes went to work with him on Saturdays, and drew pictures of trucks, and cleaned his desk for extra allowance.

Once, we pulled up to his office, and there sat a classy, bright yellow go-cart with a fiberglass Jeep body. So cool. It gleamed as one of the few material things I ever really wanted to own. Every week I received my three dollar allowance for my chores. I faithfully stashed away every cent for that Jeep, and marked off my financial ledger. I needed over one hundred of these three dollar allowances.

My green-brown eyes shone with excitement and my heart warmed, whenever I daydreamed about driving that speedy little Jeep. Directly behind our modest residence, beyond the clothesline and the school yard, a cloistered woods spanned into coppery dirt roads and welcoming verdant trees. I imagined driving into that vast expanse, the bronze dust clouds behind me. I could almost feel the soft intensity of whispery wind on my face, pigtails flying high, leaving all the pain of life behind.

Somehow, Grace or providence stepped in, because one day the Jeep showed up in *our driveway*, even though I knew my ledger still demanded dozens more three-dollar increments.

I was so excited that finally I could begin to take adult form and expression in the world—though some part of me already knew myself as a grown-up.

To my surprise, my sleek automobile didn't go as fast as I had anticipated. One hot sunny afternoon, I sat down in my blue-jean overalls, squinting in the bright noon glare, in serious discussion with my brother about this.

I had his full attention on this major life problem. I could feel it; he was behind me. And he came through with flying colors. He showed me how to take the governor off.

"What is that thing called again...?"

"The *governor*, Ann Marie," came the patient reply.

Then it was almost too fast, too wild, too scary... *until I got used to it...*

It sent thrilling, joyful chills down my spine.

And one Christmas I asked for this huge, pink stuffed-animal turtle. And Ella the Turtle showed up under the tree. I imagined myself as *The* Turtle Queen, and everyone in my queen-dom shone as so supremely happy.

Somehow—among the stresses, insecurities, defeats—those few bright moments popped up like vibrant purple tansies of surprise, in an unwatered garden of dirt and weeds.

"*I want a divorce*" changed everything.

He may as well have said, "*I want a hurricane.*" Or perhaps he meant, "I want liberation from that which is binding and diluting me."

Did they deeply inquire within if this path would truly serve them or their children? Did they assess how to provide the maximum stability and relationship cohesiveness? If done with hostility and in chaos, then when the family bond burned, would they, would we, be able to find our Phoenix wings to rise out of the ashes?

In this case, the path didn't feel right to me. The adults here— Mom and Dad, their new dating partners—were all running from what they couldn't face. They didn't know how to create what they needed. Really, they were running away from themselves and the Divine Presence.

That's all any of us ever can really do, until we come *Home*.

Home in the Heart… Father Ahavah… Eternal Love.

Not fully in union with that, they couldn't find the peace *inside*.

I empathically absorbed the contents of their pain. I even detected the bitter and indignant emotional force in their tone of voice, as they sang popular hit songs on the radio.

Dad's Rod Stewart rendition of "Maggie I wished I'd never seen your fa-a-a-ce," made me wince, as I could feel that his Maggie was my mom. I welled up with Mom's sadness, felt in my own heart, as she parroted with sorrow, Olivia Newton John. She communicated with my father though the invisible airwaves: "Have you never been mellow… have you never *tr-i-i-i-ed* to find the comfort from *ins-i-i-i-de you*… have you never let *someone else be str-o-o-o-ng*?"

Even my dear widowed Grandma, after living alone for years, hotly sang at her new partner "You can't even run your own life… I'll be damned if you'll run mine!" I exclaimed, "Grandma! That sounds so terrible!" And my Grandma, whom I loved, had *such pain* on her face as she carefully explained how controlled she felt by her partner and her plans to leave him. I felt deep sorrow for her pain, her loneliness, and for how much we all seem to struggle in this world.

And all the while, all we wish to do is love and be loved!

I took on their pain, until I couldn't distinguish their emotional pain bodies and belief systems from my own.

Life deteriorated into a progressively more unstable, polarized, and heavy maze.

I waited for this impending divorce as if spiraling down toward some awful thing. I failed to give voice to what I witnessed. It felt similar to feeling the strong winds blow, seeing the sky darken to blue-black, hearing the clapping thunder, seeing the sparks of lightening flash—yet the rainfall never seems to come. When would this divorce happen?

One night, my father announced he was taking my brother and I for a drive. It was one of the *bad moments*, but it wasn't sudden, unexpected, or violent. At first, I didn't recognize it.

I guess my brother *was there* for *one* of the bad moments.

The three of us climbed into the truck, lined up, *staring straight ahead.*

No one looked at anyone.

No eye contact, no looking at anyone's body language.

I questioned why we were going for a drive at this time of night. We *never ever* just drove. I wanted to go home.

I wondered if this *drive-to-nowhere* sprang up because we had no money to go anywhere. Dad previously told stories about times they were so poor all they could afford was to go out for a drive. And he shared about the more destitute times when they couldn't even afford gas.

My stomach hurt.

Dad stared straight ahead and said, "We are getting a divorce." My brother stared straight ahead and started to cry. I stared straight ahead—confused, afraid, sad. I still didn't know what divorce was or what it meant. I did know that when Dad said the word to my Mom, his voice was as hard and final as an iron wall.

When I saw my big brother cry, I got scared.

I didn't know what divorce was, but I knew I didn't want us all to get one.

We all drove down the road, staring straight ahead.

***

A few weeks later I came home and saw Mom crying as she pushed Dad's tall chest of drawers into my brother's room. Brother was helping her, his cheeks wet with tears.

My throat choked up and I walked into my room. There was a note from Dad saying he was leaving me his tennis racket. I sat with the wooden racket and watched my Mom and brother round the bend, past my bedroom door, pushing that heavy chest, heaving sobs from their chests.

I realized that it wasn't a coincidence that I had spent last night with a friend and didn't get home until after my father was gone.

I had come home all excited to tell Dad about their ice cream. We always scooped ours with a round scoop. To my delighted astonishment, my girlfriend's dad, who had jet-black straight hair and matching sideburns, sliced our ice cream into big rectangles and proudly served them to us with his big smiles. I wanted my dad to make ice cream slabs too.

I walked home that morning in the tall grass, the wind whipping locks of honey-brown hair softly across my face. Squinting in the bright golden sun, I reasoned that if he could figure out how to build a picnic table with his own hands, and he knew how to fix cars and make the engines turn over, then he could make chocolate, strawberry, and vanilla rectangles stack up like Legos.

Dad knew how to fix a lot of things, but he didn't know how to fix a heart or a feeling.

And he didn't know how to say "I am sorry" and he didn't know how to make his little girl feel loved, or safe, or sweet, or happy. He didn't know how to make his daughter feel like… *his daughter*.

Maybe, deep down, some part of him did know. But he just couldn't find his way to let that part of himself live and breathe, to find its lungs and express its voice, and to feel its wonderment.

I stared at the tennis racket. I would keep scooping ice cream in circular balls, while he began ruining saucepans, burning chocolate pudding, in his bachelor apartment on the other side of town.

Now

Now, when I reflect on this, I can feel each person's pain. The sensitive, creative, mystical little girl—longing for innocence, safety, and love—but perceiving herself as deeply abandoned, swirled into deep pain and insecurity from the unconscious behaviors thrown at her. *Forgotten.*

I feel the pre-teen brother—needing a loving, nurturing, strong masculine figure and a self-assured Mother—his tenderness turning to rebellion and independence much too early. *Lost.*

I feel the depressed, unfulfilled mother sink into rejection and overwhelm. *Defeated.*

And I feel the tension of the father—the pressing burden of life demanding more, as he starts over again. *Bitter.*

At times, each person feels like character—no one more personal or impersonal than another. At other times, Ann feels most real. More and more often, there is no sense of being Ann or any person or personality, but of being *Spirit Presence.*

Compassion pervades this being, and a passion for us all, en masse, to deeply understand and love each other... to remember, and come *Home to Divinity, as Light.*

Revisiting the past is like reading a story, yet having a keen memory and awareness of the nuances, thoughts, emotions, and patterns.

It's like watching a character in a movie, while hooked up to an apparatus that allows one to think, feel, and *be* the emotions, vibrations and neuro-chemical system of the main character.

It's as if "something" far beyond a person, woman or little girl experienced all this.

This is about Us.

This is our *journey*, from the wounded masculine to the Divine Masculine, from a personal "me" to the Heart of Father God. It is our *journey* from the suppressed or abused feminine to the Divine Feminine, the honoring of Mother Mary, or what we see as the Eternal Mothering aspect of God. It is the remembrance of masculine/feminine as one harmoniously unified essence, as One Infinite Unified Life—alive as holy adoration, and at rest as simple joy.

Most of all this is our summons to *show up*— here and now— *for* and *as* the direct remembrance of *Original Creation*, far beyond these dreams and dramas of separation, of fear, of "me," of "mine."

It is a mandate—a call—to sacredness. We have no more time to be insensitive, unaware, sloppy, numb, apathetic, in "survival mode," or in any former unconscious mode of operation.

We have no more time for unsustainable patterns, selfish trespasses, or lack of responsibility for clearing our own emotional storage bins and releasing life-crushing beliefs.

We have no more time to fail to communicate, or to make eye contact, or to open the heart with compassion. We have no more time to dismiss solidarity and trust, and to superficially evade deep, committed relationships.

We have no more time to ignore the deep existential crisis of the hearts of all beings, crying out for freedom from suffering and for a sane, sustainable world.

We cannot solve the fragmentation and chaos at the level of fragmentation and chaos. We rise above the perceptions of this collective pool of ancient problems by *Being Presence, by Being Peace*. We open to and abide as that *Reality*.

Part of the deep insecurity that haunted my childhood, and lingered as a ghost in my adulthood, was seeing that those I loved lacked insight into the weight, and the cost, of trespassing against themselves and others.

When it comes to making life-altering decisions, especially involving young children—and tender hearts of any age—it's best to fully investigate within to discern the highest course. One must be sure that the pathway really serves everyone concerned, not just, *Does this action serve the personal "me" character?* Insight comes from surrendering—to hear, to know—how Spirit Presence is reflecting Itself, how Divine Light is expressing.

My parents, the family guides, lost their way when the conditioned, personal self wasn't getting what it thought it wanted.

Loss of focus creates unrest and distress.

It creates stress twenty-four hours a day, not just the during the occasional "acting out." When those we love are not focused on and as the higher *Spirit Reality,* on a higher unified purpose, we feel the insecurity, the unrest, the lack of solidarity.

Lack of devotion weakens us…

Until our passion is so strong that we focus, softly, inexorably, with the momentum of divine strength. We stop fixating on those who are wavering—or on the unsustainable structures—and we hone in on *Reality*. We directly experience the *Essential Spirit Self*. This *Aliveness in God,* awakens so potently that we serve as a lighthouse for those who meet in this golden cathedral of peace. We sing celestial symphonies in one chorus, in the soft radiance of the true *Heart's Home*.

We now awaken as Father Ahavah! Father Spirit Love!

Never alone, not ever forgotten. Rather than the absence of any person, we spring alive as the *Presence, Eternally Here Now, Father Ahavah,* one with and as *That.*

Experiential Aplication

I Exist As the Sacred Immensity Without Walls,

Immortal Lungs of Heaven's Voice as

Self Complete Happiness Presence

Contemplate each phrase, as more and more deeply, you relax and feel peace. This is not a learning, acquiring, or a becoming. It is a resting... opening... remembering... being. Simply remember that which *You* already exist *As*.

Though there are many phrases, realize this is not a complex or complicated practice. Let each step simply guide you to a deepening experiential awareness.

Father Ahavah Contemplative Prayer

- Inhale and exhale slowly and fully
- Allow the breath to breathe you, as you relax deeply into spacious peace
- Allow the entire body to relax, more and more fully and deeply
- Feel a soft, enveloping safety... ease... peace

- Have an intention to welcome, feel and release emotional storage around divorce, relationship separations, relationship distancing
- Without suppressing it, or attaching to it, simply allow to surface any unresolved feeling of loss... void... sadness
- Sit with these feelings as sensations, allowing the breath to seem to breathe them into an expansion, rather than a contraction... on each exhale release sensations into the surrounding space... until you only breathe out compassion
- Rather than a tense or contracted personal "me" with a tense or contracted emotion be the *Presence of Peace*, intuiting a ray of peace within and beneath emotions
- Be the *Eternal Peace* the emotion sits within, and be the peace within the emotion... not analyzing this or mentally attempting this... simply have attention and awareness of being the *Peace Presence* the emotion seems to arise to, present itself to... and realize that a spark of this same *Presence lies beneath-within* the emotion
- Rest as being the space of love, and see this same space of love, right there where the emotion seems tight and contracted
- Allow that seed of love and peace to expand and expand, as the emotional contraction releases
- This means sitting with the feeling as it is, and then contemplating that you, as *Spirit Presence*, exist where the emotion is felt
- Within the sensation of emotion, *Peace Is*
- Resting as that Peace, let the contracted emotion open or collapse into nothingness

- See the emotion as an ocean wave, and see the ocean of space, of peace within the wave, and the wave thus "collapses" or "dissolves" back into the ocean of peace... yet it was the ocean of peace the entire time
- Upon the ocean of Spacious Presence, a wave of disturbance or emotion seems to arise, yet it falls back into the ocean, as if the superficial wave never was
- In that way, emotions simply flow at a comparatively surface level, without becoming stuck or stored or suppressed
- Feel this, or if it's not easy to feel this, then simply contemplate this spacious openness and relax
- Feel emotions as purely as sensations... without words, or thoughts, or commentary
- Simply feel the sensations and release
- Have awareness of stored emotions from "staring straight ahead syndrome" (the times we shut down without expression, or we had to "keep going" so we did not have the capacity to deeply feel)
- *Softly Be*... rest, go softer and softer... emotions unlayer... feel spacious *Peace* beneath the emotions
- Be aware of feeling any numbness or of suppressing the voice
- Feel this numbness... this being shut down... this locking up inside—as much as you do... let it go as much as you can...
- Have an awareness of the Divine Love, changeless and deep
- And that upon that, like surface waves, you can have either side of a polarity human affection or distancing,

human marriage or divorce, human sentiment or abandonment

- We wish to move beyond the "good" side of the polarity, and the "bad" side of the polarity
- This moves us out of ups and downs, and good and bad, and unstable life
- Feel more passion to live as the *Eternal FatherAhavah Love*, than any temporary changing emotion or experience, than either side of an opposite experience
- Open to let attachment or belief in either side of the polarity to grow lighter (release back and forth)
- For example, release affection and let go... release its opposite end of the pole, such as distancing or rejection and also let that go
- Then feel and release human affection to drop down to *Father Ahavah Eternal Love*, then again release emotions from distancing or rejection... and rest as Father Ahavah Eternal Love
- Feel any emotions that arise of separation, or grief from divorce, break ups or abandonment, estrangement... feel it as much as you do... gently let go... take a moment for this... rest in the Eternal Love beneath it
- Then have awareness of any feelings of sentiment, attachment, affections, as much as you do, and then also release that feeling... rest in this... in the Eternal Love beneath it
- Again feel any arising residue of separation and abandonment, let go and relax into Divine Love, Spirit Love beneath those feelings

- Then again feel any arising sense of affection, sentiment, attachment, release those feelings to the underlying Divine Love that is beyond changing emotion
- Thus back and forth, release both sides of the polarity of emotions... affection vs. abandonment... sentiment vs. separation... human love vs. human hate...
- Polarity or duality process is a huge key to oneness with *Father Ahavah*
- See this as a magnificent support process in identifying as Spirit Presence, rather than personal "me" — open to feel a passionate commitment to this process
- Have awareness of the *Oneness with God Presence* beneath the emotional separation feeling and the *Oneness with God Presence* beneath the emotional closeness feeling — the *Spirit Oneness* prior to all changing emotion, that is changeless Spirit Love
- Pause to accept the immense relief and astounding ineffable peace of *Eternal Love* that is not ever withheld, does not change... imminent... intimate... present... here... now!
- Again, feel the energy, the thought-emotion-sensation of divorce, or separation, or estrangement... as much as you do, and softly sit with those feelings as sensations, allowing them to soften, release and fade
- Realize that right there, before or beneath those emotions, you exist as *Unconditional Love Happiness* beneath all sensations
- Feel the sense of affection, sentiment, attachment on a mental emotional level, and drop down deeper to the more rarefied unchanging Presence

- Know *Spirit Self,* as *Self-Complete Happiness*... happening within

- If you cannot feel it at any given moment, simply contemplate *already existing* as one with *God, Self-Complete, surrender to this Eternal Union*

- Each contemplation as *Spirit Reality* is an investment in eternal treasures, an investment in true eternal happiness, an investment in reverence of that which *Created You*

- Rest in this each day, each hour, each timeless Now instant—*Self-Complete Happiness, subtle yet potent joyous peace*

- Identify more as this *Self-Complete Happiness Presence,* than as any thoughts, feelings, or experiences of aloneness or separation (or experiences of affection, sentiment, or attachment)

- Alive as *Self-Complete Happiness, One with Father Ahavah!*

Selah!

Chapter Five

Lost

From I Lost What I Was
To Glorious Ineffable Essential Purpose

Then

In elementary school I preferred Nancy Drew mystery books to dolls, and creative projects (drawing by the trees, making forts in nature) to coloring books. I held an affinity for reading a Bible, or even a dictionary, more than to perusing comic books, or chatting about trivia at ice cream socials.

In my teens, I had a natural high intelligence, and an impassioned quest for truth and answers. This resulted in high grades and performing well on exams, regardless of emotional states. When I hurt inside, I studied anyway. When I needed nurturing, I kept looking straight ahead and worked harder.

I coped with emotional duress by trying harder, studying more, and proving my worth through overdoing. Though I had despaired of receiving my father's approval and attentive interest, some habitual mechanism kept kicking in, prodding me to earn or gain his love. The more he withheld himself, the more anxiously I attempted to prove I could be his priority.

Futility.

From elementary school to high school I placed my straight "A" report card on the dining room table... waiting for his response. And... waiting...waiting. I received more genuine interest and accolades from my professors. Though I experienced mild validation in that, I longed for my father's affirmation of my gifts, life purpose... and *value for just being*.

Disappointment.

At times, my highest creative gifts spiraled deep within, buried in stuck circles, trapped in the mazes of disapproval and indifference.

Nonetheless, that immaculately wild impulse that grants the power to transcend any person or condition of this world, ignited a fiery spark of devotion to make a difference in the world. I studied in order to one day give wisdom back to the world. I glided through school like a dolphin in its synchronistic path of grace, arcing through the sea.

I won a contest titled "The student most gifted to influence America with his/her writing". Something pulsed within me to engage in a life vocation as an author. As a young girl and woman, *author* resonated as part of *who I was*, not just the calling I had in life. It arose as a destined unction to express a message of sacredness and relevance at an epic time in humanity.

After the traumas of the teen years, it required total faith to believe in salvaging a life purpose. One day, out of the blue, my father asked what I wanted to do "when I grew up." I felt halfway hopeful and cautiously excited that he was even asking. A secret smile stole across my heart.

I spontaneously felt a radiant determination to share. I so deeply yearned for two things: his *validation and his attentive involvement.*

Quick as a flash, with pride, unabashed joy, and crystalline heart smile, I cried out, "I want to be an author!"

I held my breath in anticipation and attentively observed every instant of his body language, expressions, and words. I felt butterflies of vulnerability in my stomach, yet rosy excitement flushing in my cheeks. I had revealed a secret of who I was, a hidden gift. That risk felt liberating and frightening at the same time. Could I trust him with this?

Breathless. Waiting.

His eyes hardened. His jaw clenched down. I felt the heat of anger and the scorn of disapproval coming off his body like steam rises from black asphalt, pelted with sudden rain on a scorching hot day.

His face contorted in aversion, as if I had just offered him a big brown pile of pungent and repugnant dog poop.

Yet, I had offered him myself.

My writing aspiration was not the offense; "I " was the offense.

Dark storm clouds swept across his face and his furious eyes flashed with impatience and disgust. He shook his head and threw his hands up as if to say, *Where did I go wrong!? What's wrong with you!? Can you ever get it right!?*

The wounded masculine energy flew out of his being like a steel plate, hitting me in the throat and choking me with shame. Once more, I sat cringing at the bottom of that ever-deepening black hole... spiraling down... to *nowhere*. I'd been there far too long, pulling ever inward, into a smaller and smaller cellar of the soul, into that old familiar musty smell of death: *unwanted and defeated*. No purpose.

I had offered him not just what I wanted to do; I had offered my father *what I was*.

Dad delivered dominating directives droning on for an hour, "You are so stupid! You will never make any money at that! You will never amount to anything. Do something else, some trade, not an author! Stupid!"

Years later, while cleaning teeth as a dental hygienist—frustrated out of my mind, depressed in my heart—I said under my breath "… not making a whole lot of money at this either, Dad."

How expensive is it to lose ourselves?

To lose our heart?

To lose our essential purpose?

When our *essential purpose* fails, when our birthright smolders in the embers and ashes of frustration's destructive heat—rather than our destiny scintillating in bonfires of creative genius—what *exactly* is the cost?

Once, when diagnosed with a life threatening illness, and experiencing exhaustion, I inquired within, *what is beneath this?* Quick as a flash the answer hotly electrified me —and coldly shrouded me—*failed essential purpose.*

Later, as an adult woman, it dawned on me: I had unwittingly allowed myself to be manipulated by men (or the unconsciousness of those around me) to give up what I most wanted to have or to express... or to be.

I envisioned my *essential purpose to tenderly blaze as a lighthouse of wisdom and joy.* But instead, I lost heart.

A few days after that insight, I realized I had not just been manipulated out of what I *wanted*; I had been manipulated out of what I *was.*

And, unaware of the magnitude of the spirit magnificence within, I unwittingly *manipulated myself* out of what I was born to express.

For many layers of reasons, my inner knowing—not only that *I* **want to be** *an author, but that I* **am** *an author; and that my creativity must be allowed to naturally express,* locked down. And the natural knowing of: *I Am Spirit Presence, one with Creator, from which the creative field arises and expresses*—grew dimmer and dimmer. My father's "You are stupid; you need a real job; you need to be someone other than you are" grew stronger and stronger.

It wasn't just that he did not agree with writing as a profession. He needlessly humiliated me. He shut down the innate fatherly instinct to nurture, validate, protect, and uplift. A more balanced way: encourage the writing gift, while exploring avenues of self-sufficiency in writing careers. Or honor the gift while discovering supplemental income generation while developing the craft. The issue had less to do with writing, than with respect, caring, joining… love.

The "I know and love myself and am happy with myself," diluted and waned. The core stress that plagues the humans: "I have to be something else *other than I was made to be,* in order to survive or be accepted" solidified, escalated.

My father disdained my true gifts, and I unconsciously swallowed his aversion. I absorbed this global lack of self-acceptance, this en masse secret dissatisfaction with self.

It wasn't just that I had little confidence to create success at what I did; I had no confidence in **what I was.**

I did not know that life could **support me** in *what I was.*

If my parent did not support who I was… did God?

Did I?

A vague underlying haunting fear spooked me, taunted me.

I tucked away my highest gifts like make-believe trinkets in a fairy tale box. It hurt too much to open the treasure chest of the self, and feel the icy cold shocks of *what I was,* vehemently shoved back in my blushing-with-embarrassment face.

The serial rejections clung to me like little leeches; sucking predators stealing life force and goodness. The frustration and grief of *lost essential purpose* stagnated in pools of tears, denied and frozen.

Blockages.

Obstacles.

Like a programmed marionette, I fulfilled life's survival requirements... disenchanted... looking straight ahead... *to nowhere.*

Not writing, rejoicing, expressing, sharing, or shining in rhythmic drumming of delight...

I learned obedience, and walked to the monotonous dirge of lost purpose; beaten down by domination, censure and ridicule. My passion for the essential purpose retreated, anesthetized to sleep. I was tricked into the common slavery of abandoning the *magnitude of what I was.*

Now

I feel impersonal compassion for the father who could not open to the magnitude of *who I was. Or who he was.*

Disconnected from nurture of his insecure places, he coped with fear by control. Rather than discover, and celebrate *what I was*, he manipulated and molded me to be something *other.*

We fear what we see as "other."

This is a core pattern of humanity, a global virus: *control.*

Humanity's ignorance: see "otherness" out there, that is *different,* and thus should be *feared...* and thus should be controlled.

That which invokes fear of losing the known, that which stretches us seemingly beyond our limits, that which tempts us to prematurely and inauthentically wrap everything up in a neat little box that we can control, is our teacher.

Pay attention to the aversions that tempt us to run.

Controlling something is running from it.

Rather than judging the shadowy devils of control… lurking… face and meet the urge to control with celestial compassion and with angelic clarity.

Every time I released even the most subtle attempt to control a situation, I experienced an immediate crisp clarity, a spontaneous soft humble grace. Suddenly unconventional solutions presented themselves, and previously hidden vistas of bright opportunity shot up like a flare.

When we control, we lose our realness.

No longer courageously real, we have to whip up the more rigid and fake version of the self.

Tenderness is lost. The Real is lost.

With his lack of trust in the spiritual and creative gifts, the primary masculine authority in my early life lacked inner assurance. Thus he failed to bequeath honor and trust to his offspring. He tried to "make me strong" by force. The more he forced, the more dominated I felt.

It spiraled. The more rejected and dominated I felt, the more my confidence nose-dived. The more my confidence deflated from abuse, the more abandoned and in need of support that I felt.

He forced me to be "independent" by the very means that creates dependence.

He unwittingly thought he drove me to be "sensible". Yet, he lost sight of the bigger losses: he pressured me to deny my intuitive knowing, crush my blossoming womanhood, and undermine the magical. I felt dejected and jaded.

The biggest loss: love.

I feel an immense compassion that he did not experience more of the sweetness of life, the support of the universe, the tender intimacy of the *Father Ahavah* Presence. Rather than judging him for not giving it to his progeny, I softly hold a sacred prayer that he know the true Eternal Father's love, in his heart.

Now peace arises in *being*... not being this or that... simply *being*.

A refreshing clear light dawns, being the beholder who acts from spiritual impulse. There is no sense of attachment to being an "author" or "therapist" or "audio creator" or "retreat facilitator" or "spiritual teacher". Author is not the first primary core of what I was or who I am, yet it is honored as secondary essential purpose —prospering through the first Essential Purpose. *Presence Is.*

There exists aliveness as the deeper *Essence,* the Essential Self. Spirit Self sings its song in this sweet, radical, surrendered beholding of Light. It shines the beauty of service, through the human life and physical form experience.

For many of us, who wish to express the more refined or rarefied aspects of the self, an initiation into rejection or resistance to that gift occurs.

Ultimately, we have a summons to establish *conviction and faith in our primary and our secondary essential purpose*—and commit to the epic life that unfolds in the golden dawning of their *merging*—independently of anyone else's thoughts, reactions or opinions.

We have our truest essential life purpose and our secondary life purpose. The truest life purpose is the direct experience of Oneness with God Presence, the remembrance of the Essential Self, Spirit.

Primary life purpose: I Exist as Eternal Spirit, One with God Light… the *Essential Self,* as lived, tangible, direct reality.

Living as that is the highest calling, and resting in that is a selfless service.

Secondary life purpose: When directly awake as *Spirit Presence,* that *Presence may* express as a fiery impulse to compassionate action, or the thundering silence of exquisitely still illumined inspiration.

Primary and secondary life purpose marry and merge: This sacred transfiguration means the *Essential Life of God Oneness,* embodies, emboldens, *em-goldens* rich service. This feels like the crisp air refreshing the landscape of life, after a noonday soothing downpour of fresh rain. Like a rushing wind, invigorating and expansive, the *Holy One, the vast God Magnificence,* reveals extraordinary miracles in the most ordinary moments. The personal-character-self surrenders, empties, trusts in and serves the Divine.

It's quietly thrilling to be the *Nothingness* and yet see it flow as the *Allness.*

Abiding as Presence, *Light,* fulfills *Life,* not the roles played or the accomplishments completed.

The heart beckons toward *The Limitless*... a call to realize boundless life without the confining borders of past beliefs. Ineffable faith, the mountain moving power of the Holy Spirit parts the red sea to open a way of safe journeys in the midst of life's storms.

And that *Sacred Presence* expresses as *Itself*... never lost... eternally changeless... as a firm foundation.

When we identified as anything other than *Original Innocence, Essential Spirit Life,* we lost what we were.

We actually do not "lose" it, we "lose" the direct experience of it.

Now we are no longer lost.

And we come *Home.*

As the Victorious Essential Purpose, ablaze.

Home.

Still Home.

As the Light.

Experiential Aplication

Alive As Self-Complete Happiness Presence

Truth is simple.

This practice does not require learning, acquiring, or trying.

Simply rest in each phrase. Close your eyes often, to rest in the practice and contemplate each unfolding aspect of the message.

See this as remembrance of the Spirit Presence, with whom you exist as One.

Father Ahavah Contemplative Prayer

- Breathe fully, deeply, slowly
- Slowly scan your body and release any tight or constricted areas as if expanding any contractions or tensions to the space around you
- Be aware of any of the lost self-expression, any buried emotions from rejection of your gifts, or failed purpose
- Allow any memories/emotions of failed essential and secondary purpose, to have permission to spontaneously surface to be met with healing *Love*
- See the memories, yet rest more attention on *Presence*

- Rest as Spirit *Presence*, upon which emotions rise and fall
- Allow thoughts to slow and quiet… not pushed away, merely not the focal point of attention… not interested in thoughts
- Notice any sense of loss, or of failed essential purpose…
- See these emotions as simply sensations, storyless arisings… merging into *Presence Love*
- Move through any fear of your brilliance, gifts, or of their greater visibility in the world
- Have awareness of the primary essential purpose: "I exist as *One With God Presence, Limitless*"
- *Open to feel Oneness with God Presence* more deeply and potently than ever before—as *The Real*
- Care more passionately about that Divine Union than anything else
- Embrace and intimately love this *Eternal One* as you shine in the exact likeness of *Supreme Creator*
- Feel the *Causeless Happiness* of spiritually based happiness… happening on the inside…
- And embrace the secondary essential purpose—the highest expression of that *Divine Presence* through the unconditioned "you" in its unique precious exquisite expression
- Rest and celebrate new life and rich depth of beauty in every expression of life
- Rest as this *Causeless Happiness Self*
- Realize the natural adoration of *Father Ahavah*
- Rest in this Essential Purpose fulfilled
- Fly free in this *Father Ahavah, Eternal Love*

אהבה

Selah!

Chapter Six

The Initiation

From Initiation Into Violence
To the Power of The Quieting

Then

Something about thirteen.

It's innocent and fluid and vulnerable.

A wild age.

A sacred age.

For me, age thirteen marked *The Initiation Into The Violence.*

At the beginning of each new school year, I tried to buy at least one new outfit. My few clothes were worn out, and the washing machines were a long walk away and demanding of coins. A new outfit meant fewer laundry trips.

However, new clothes also meant spending money.

I dreaded asking my father for money.

Whenever I needed or wanted something, I pondered for days whether to go without, try to earn the money, or go through *the ordeal* of asking for money.

His reluctances, his harsh responses, and his anger at the request felt demoralizing.

I felt a knot of dread in my stomach, the pressure of shame in my head, from being an uncelebrated burden. It felt like stinging slaps to my heart, a humiliating losing face... *rejection.*

I longed for warmth, affection, connection, and inclusion. Yet I wandered, lost among "family" snowdrifts—hanging my head and walking quickly—hoping things warmed up before my unshed tears froze my heart to death.

At some deep level, the imprint of "undeserving burden" branded me in a way that seemed un-erasable.

I wished for one school outfit, but it was becoming an *ordeal*. The pressure of shame and frustration grew stronger. I decided to find a way to create my own money.

I found a babysitting job close by. When I had enough dollars for at least one outfit, I set out on foot for the mall, my proudly-won earnings in my hands. The path ran parallel to Highway 19, and offered open space, except for one small patch of woods behind a Ramada Inn.

I found a pair of white pants that I loved more than blue jeans, and a white and orange striped shirt. Shopping by myself, I felt lonely, but also relieved.

In the late afternoon I began the walk home, and soon reached the edge of the small woods behind the hotel. I walked quickly in broad daylight, the shopping bag with my one little outfit casually swinging by my side.

I did not see this as risky or dangerous. Just across the small wooded space, an open field led to the blacktop parking lot of our apartment complex. We lived in the very back row of about a dozen buildings.

I'd trudged halfway through the woods when suddenly a man appeared. He was wiry and short, with light brown hair and a shaky nervousness to his stride and his countenance.

He passed me by and I kept walking, looking straight ahead. I fantasized about wearing my white pants and orange top on the first day of school, making new school friends.

Suddenly the stranger's nervousness, which masked violent rage and sinister criminality, was all around me—smothering me, choking me, shaking me, and trying to throw me to the ground.

I screamed the instant he grabbed me from behind, but he already had both hands over my mouth. He violently shook my head, pressing my face down, clamping my jaws shut, while growling, "Shut up, shut up, shut up," over and over.

I *knew* he was trying to rape me.

I felt terrified. But also an unstoppable force rose up within my being, avowing *"Not on my life!"*

I knew—*no matter what*—he was not going to *touch me there*. He was not going to violate me that way; I would fight him to the death.

I inwardly called out, *God, God!* again and again. Without a thought, I instinctively called upon that which I knew was *all Presence, and all* **Holy.**

I wasn't calling out to a concept of God, or having a thought, or saying "Oh My God." My whole being was inwardly, silently screaming, emanating with intense force and passion: *God!* **My** *God! Reveal Your Self! Here! Now!*

The odds were against me. But somehow in the midst of the raging battle and inner cries, I knew I was *heard*.

It was the first time in my life in "this world" I sensed I was truly <u>heard</u> at such a deep, sacred level in the actual moment of the violence.

No one in my physical surroundings heard my muffled screams. No person saw the struggle.

It was the middle of the afternoon in broad daylight, behind a large hotel full of guests, next to one of our busiest highways and close to a large apartment complex with hundreds of tenants.

No one saw? No one heard?

In the invisible realms, *more real than all the visible ones*—in some unexplainable way that I did not understand, I knew I was seen and known and *heard*.

We struggled and fought.

An inspiration flashed: *Get your teeth into his hands.* I struggled with all my force to pry his hands off me and to sink my teeth into him.

I felt my tooth hit his skin and I bit and fought with everything I had. In the split second his hand withdrew from my bite, I released a blood-curdling scream, a nanosecond before his knife appeared.

He recoiled just long enough for me to start sprinting out of his reach.

As the knife flashed, I fled, and called out to any living, breathing thing that would *hear me.*

No one came.

But I had my miracle—Divine Grace, like a halo of power all around me—and I ran fast as lightning.

My little package was long forgotten, left behind in the dirt. The bag lay in the silence of the woods that had just witnessed the cold hush of innocence violated. Only the trees and birds had heard the shrieks of the feminine soul, tormented by violent hands that had forgotten the natural way.

I will never ever forget that run.

I ran in horror, with immense pounding fear. Every part of me hurt. My ripped pierced ears flowed blood; my body bore the wounds of countless scrapes and bruises. A throbbing excruciating pain flooded my head, and a paralyzing contraction locked up my jaw, throat and neck.

A thought quickly pulsed: *God, please let there be someone home!*

At that moment, I was just running for my life, but any semblance of childhood was over. I was initiated into the grip of violence.

As I ran, panting with exhaustion and screaming loudly for help, I silently pleaded in my heart, *God, let there be someone home...*

Let there be someone home... let there be someone home...

Please God, let there be someone home!

My father's girlfriend heard me from far away. She stood there with the front door open, looking scared out of her wits, as I rounded the bend at full speed.

She called my father on the phone. Her voice shook. And I thought, *He's at work and he might not be able to come now.*

But he arrived faster than I thought was humanly possible. And somehow, in that moment, I felt that he loved me.

He was deeply distraught and he had come home lightning fast. He *must* love me.

At the police station, I earned the title of "Little Tiger." Apparently this man was a serial rapist and I was the only one who had gotten away. One of the officers looked surprised; another looked at me with genuine pride and admiration.

I knew it was *Divine Grace*, but I let myself feel proud anyway. The pride evaporated quickly as hot tears flowed and my hypervigilant nervous system spiked again.

I endured drawing his face and looking through photo-boxes of sex offenders, rapists, and violent criminals. At one point, I exclaimed," I can't believe how many of these are old men!."

The officers looked at each other, squirming, but said nothing.

I felt disgust and revulsion looking at these criminals' faces.

And then there was the lineup.

I asked again and again, "If I look at these men behind the glass, are you sure they cannot see me? Are you really sure?"

After that *Initiation,* my every waking moment was dramatically shifted. That vice grip was so tight, so pervasive, so wickedly tenacious, that I had to cling to Grace—to the *Reality of the Tenderness of God*—even more inexorably, to ever break free.

Even my neurological system had altered to resonate to the ever-playing mantra of trauma alert, and school became a nightmare.

During *The Violence,* the perpetrator had crept up behind me after having passed by. In the crowded hallways at school, shaking and whipping my head around every time someone passed by, finally I'd run into the bathroom and shut myself in a stall and cry.

I stayed home from school for weeks at a time, cowering in the closet any time I heard a noise. Once I was in the hallway when I heard something, and I darted into a hard, empty bathtub and hid there all day.

During the long nights alone, I would lock my bedroom door and listen to make sure no one was trying to break in.

Eventually my bladder would grow so full that crossed the hall to the bathroom. Time and again, I heard a noise and grew too terrified to come out. Many nights I spent half the night on the bathroom floor, afraid to cross the hall back to my bedroom.

Eventually my father came home from dinner, the sports pub, or the ball game. He eventually figured out what was happening, as I sheepishly came out of the bathroom, all scared and sleepy. He laughed and said, "I would get you a gun but I'm afraid you would shoot me."

It wasn't funny and I wasn't laughing.

I didn't know about PTSD (Post-Traumatic Stress Disorder) or therapy. No one took me for psychological or medical treatment.

The time came that I knew I couldn't live in this isolating, trembling hell. Fear filled my being. My neurological system wired to fight or flight. I lay awake at night with flashbacks, shaking alone in my bed, tears spilling over my tender skin.

There is little one can do out in the world if you're terrified every time someone walks past. Even one day, sitting in the bathroom, a giant spider walked past and scared the daylights out of me.

If someone walked by, I had to spin around to make sure they weren't coming from behind to attack me. No matter how many times I told myself they were not, the sweating and trauma feeling welled up, and I *had* to look.

My body became a prison.

But by *Divine Grace*, during my contemplations all alone in those closets, and bathtubs, and bedrooms, I received the most exquisite and powerful techniques to shift from trauma into feeling safe, feeling *Divine Compassion*, feeling love.

Once I received an inspiration to focus on my fast heart beat as if God was there. Nothing happened. Then I had an impression... **Trust this... trust that Father God of Love is there, is here, is what really happens.** I collapsed into that like a flower collapsing into a perfect rose bud, empty of pain, and then expanded out now potently flowering in spirit love. It involved a total deep relinquishing "let go" of the memory, and a soft opening to the instantaneous immensity of *Father God Love, Father Ahavah*. And my racing heartbeat slowed. My cheeks and face felt aglow with Light. My eyes shone with radiant peace.

I did the same focused and spacious slowing with my breath, thoughts, emotions. I collapsed into a total let go of suffering, thought, emotion, pain, like a rag doll. And dropping into the deep ocean of *Holy Spirit Love, Presence Light*, I opened and radiated compassion and love.

The initiation into violence dissolved into the embracing, expansive *Quieting of Father Spirit Love*.

Now

If a thirteen-year-old girl meets with wise eldership and protection, her life unfolds as spontaneously joyful and calmly stable.

In many cultures, thirteen marks the beginning of a five-year transition from childhood to adulthood. It marks the time of planting roots and initial wing-testing of freedom's flight. Thirteen pivots us, as we learn to navigate from dependence to integrated interdependence, and from self-focus to caring solidarity with others.

If this threshold to womanhood or manhood has wise eldership, this supports sacred reverence of Creator, awareness of the spiritual nature of self. As the young teen learns to balance receiving with mature responsibility, he or she blossoms with creativity and contribution.

But, for some *deeply called ones,* 13 marks *Initiation into Trauma.*

If the trauma is handled with denial, unconsciousness, or inner running, either by her and/or her elders, it scars a young woman's (or young man's) life; hiding the *true self.* The trauma shatters the innate expression of reverence, joy, and giftedness.

However, if at the time of the trauma, or later in life, the he or she consciously surrenders to a path of deep emotional excavation, spiritual inquiry, and *God Oneness,* then the *initiated one* emerges as more deep, soft, bold and real. The one initiated into trauma then emerges as a *Liberated One.*

One with Divine Presence. Free.

I am a very different being than the terrified thirteen-year-old. Now, my neurological system is calmer, at ease. Even if I live alone, I feel secure and safe. If faced with a threat, such as an attempted break-in at my house, I usually stay calm, and my nervous system quickly rebalances in certainty and peace. Identity remains as Presence.

When bodily pain arises, the discomfort dissipates in contemplation, and it does not impede my productivity. My life vibrantly unfolds; it is a vital, generative life of compassionate service.

The techniques that I intuitively received though Grace, as well as my commitment to a path of emotional excavation, have transformed the way I experience and respond to the threat of violence.

These same methods developed into the processes that I have shared with countless beings—in my work as a psychotherapist, spiritual mentor, and seminar teacher—to support liberation from deep trauma.

Often a student or client exclaims: "This is astoundingly powerful; it saved my life. That's what a PhD will do for you." I smile and nod. I clearly found that a PhD didn't do much. The true gold came from shivering with fear, huddled up in the closet, and finding that the only way out of *the unbearableness* was to go within—into the sweet potent rivers of *Spirit's Grace* that is the only true elixir.

The holy grail came from dying into the holiness, surrendering into the sacredness, and awakening as the ocean of Divine adoration that is agony's only trustworthy answer.

***

One day I felt a call to travel to India. *By myself.*

Given my history, that journey proved a perfect opportunity to excavate my fears. Despite meticulous preparations, after forty hours of traveling, famished and thirsty, at three in the morning I stood outside the airport in Chennai in the dark. I searched among the crowd of drivers for my name on a sign. Prior to the flight, I took great care to ensure a reputable taxi driver waited there for me.

My heart sank as I realized that my driver had not come. I felt vulnerable and helpless as I observed the throng of men trying to corral me into their cars, which are not marked as taxis. After praying, I intuitively knew which stranger's car to enter to transport me to my hotel.

I had also arranged to have a working cell phone. It never worked the entire trip, leaving me no way to call for assistance.

No taxi waiting.

No phone.

Middle of the night.

No one speaking English.

Far from home.

Alone.

Yet, not alone.

Presence felt as Golden Light.

My driver, who I hoped was a legitimate cabbie, sped like a maniac through the back roads of run-down neighborhoods, with dilapidated old houses and half-naked men in loin cloths warming themselves around barrels of fire. Once in my hotel room, I turned the key to lock myself safely inside when I heard a gunshot outside the door. I had arrived.

A few days later, in contemplative prayer, in a safe, secluded forest, a deep awareness arose: ineffable silence of *Oneness with God Presence*. God Is. My heart warmed in that radiance, as Creator Light, as pure Immaculate Divine Love.

The direct experience of Reality deepened, in potent realization: *I exist as One with the Light of God Presence.* An eternal remembrance of existing as Eternal *Spirit, one with the Original Father Love, in the beginning...* pulsed in subtle and refined wonderment and ecstatic holy joy.

An hour later, while walking among crowds, I saw a group of people coming toward me. An unfathomable peace arose, as if those walking toward me were columns of light—they existed as the same Light I had felt in prayer—and a soft message intoned: "People are not bodies moving toward me who could reject me."

I poignantly realized that since early childhood, every single day of my life, my body-mind persona had lived unconsciously—mostly on a subtle imperceptible level—seeing other people as separate bodies moving toward me.

The "me" that felt separate saw people through a filter that *always* carried the threat of rejection. Since then, as a practicing psychotherapist and spiritual teacher, I discovered that same imprint in my clients' and students' unconscious conditioning, and also in the humans on a global level.

A soft tear of gentle recognition flowed at the immense relief and the stunning beauty of perceiving "persons" as columns of love and light.

In silent peace, the awareness deepened: *"People are not bodies moving toward me that can reject me."* My fear of bodies, of people, dissolved.

***

We do not have to suffer emotional abuse, physical abuse, or violence to hold fear or apprehension about navigating in a world of people, of persons, of events.

We may unconsciously fear disapproval, rejection, not belonging, losing control in relationships, being unloved or unwanted.

We may consciously or unconsciously feel dependent on persons for love, nurturing, security, survival, or resources to thrive.

Really see and feel in all your being: "*Eternal Spirit, I Exist as That — This Instant.*"

Have a deep knowing that God Is.

And that "*Is*" is infinite, unfathomable good.

As *One with Creator, you exist as Self-Complete.*

The *Spirit Life* cannot be damaged, wounded, or traumatized.

When we deeply and spontaneously feel alive as this *Spirit Life*, we discover the only true rest that purifies, illumines, and "divinizes" the psyche, the physiology, the mentality. It allows us to experience *Primordial Peace*, which is *Eternal Peace*, joy at rest.

Christ said, "*My Peace* is not of this world. *My Peace* I leave with you." He distinguished between the peace of the changing world, and the *Peace* of a more real and potent essence than the world of persons, places, things, thoughts, and emotions.

Christ's *My Peace* refers to *God Peace, Eternal Peace, the Primordial Original Peace* not of this world — *prior to* this world, continuing *during* this world, and *after* this world. This peace arose beyond this world or its appearances, yet Christ stated it as being known and felt by Him and those in communion with Him, *while in this world*. Not later after a human death — here now, in this world, we come come alive in communion with that *Eternal Father Ahavah Peace.*

Our whole being pulsing as *Father Ahavah Peace*, feeling the christening of Christ's Peace, a benediction of strength while in this world, yet beyond this world — softly penetrates deep enough to erase imprints of terror, post-traumatic stress, and the initiation into violence.

Spirit Presence Peace.

Nothing else truly goes deep enough.

Although at times anger arises, or strong commanding words and actions are called for in this world; the initiation into violence sparked the radical surrender to the ineffable sacredness of *Divine Tenderness.*

When knowing Self as *Spirit Presence*, I experience the most immaculate sweetness, bestowing love, breathtaking innocence, and kind intelligence.

In the midst of this, later in life, painful memories resurfaced, as if flushing to the surface the deepest final layers of anguish. These reactions were sparked by changes in my relationship with my former partner. At first, nothing would alleviate the intensity of the arising waves of emotion.

Paul did not support—in fact, he sharply criticized—my inspiration to write, especially about spiritual themes. He grew hotly defensive about both his hidden alcohol habit and also of his unkind behavior while under its desensitizing influence. All of this triggered any remaining remnants of father wounds, as if someone had picked open a scab and then drove a knife deep into the wound. *The* pain arose, along with *the* global pain of humanity, as my once loving and supportive partner cut me with cruelty.

One night, I noticed the pain arise, and allowed it to dissolve into *Presence.* Sitting *As Spirit Awareness,* a rich, glorious canticle flowed in an astounding outburst of *One Love.* I invisibly, inwardly sensed the high vibration of the song, without knowing the tune or words. It felt soft, quieting, yet blazing with Divine Love. Then, I sounded the melody, in sacred vowel tones. And then words flowed within, in cadence with the melody. As I toned and sang, a wave of tender love—from, to and as—the Divine, one inseparable totality of bliss and completion, engulfed and dissolved all pain. The canticle flowed like a river of grace.

Suffering evaporated and holiness-joy emerged, shimmering and sacred.

The realization of *"people are not bodies moving toward me who can reject me"* came home in even a deeper way. A personal sense of the "me" character dissolved. Only Light remained.

The personal "me" character emptied.

An immense emptying arose as *The Emptiness*.

That Emptiness Sat with Itself, needing and wanting nothing else.

And that Emptiness could be as it was, with no need to form any form. Or Emptiness could seem to flow into physical formation, reflective of Heaven's way.

The innocence of *The Emptiness* emerged as the conception of *The Quieting*.

The Quieting reveals Self as One with God Presence, Ineffable Holiness, Profound Peace. It is the sacred emptiness in which nothing needs to form: "I Exist as God Presence, Living Light." Yet any beautiful form may spring into expression at any spontaneous instant.

Many miracles became evident in "this life" and in "those lives" around.

A realization from many years prior came home more deeply than ever before. Walking beside the blue-green cascade of white-capped ocean waves, I felt the deep completion in union with God. I heard the still small voice whisper: *"There are no persons."* Instead of "persons," I saw *Divine Light* where they appeared. They seemed to be individualized forms of *Spirit Presence*.

The message meant: abide so deeply complete in God Presence, that no person, thing or event of this world, has distraction power to take you out of this abiding; persons are not persons in the way you think. Stay free.

A "person" is simply this spark or column of God Light at the true core—seemingly covered with layers of conditioning, thoughts, emotions, circumstances, beliefs, and identifications—that shift and change. All that is really there is the eternal *Presence*, and that *Presence* is only love.

Saints and sages have been known for eons as transparencies for God. They have surrendered to the emptiness. And in that emptiness of personal self, and emptiness of addictive focus on this world, the *Father Ahavah Light* shines through.

When the sacred adoration proves more real than the violence, the violence within beings and on the planet will wane to zero power; seen as having no actual life of its own. We have a holy mandate to see through trespasses, to see beyond the crisis of unsustainability, to transcend the tsunami of the superficial, and to awaken as the ocean of profound peace.

We are called to focus on, feel, and embody *the Sacred Tenderness*.

Be this *Sacred Tenderness*, with humility and clarity observe the shadow elements—anger, hatred, fear, pain, or trauma—arising in you.

Allow the heart to break open into the emptying—and behold these dense "energetics" unlayering. The releasing of ancient global trauma imprints, does not have to take long at this point of humanity's critical epic hour.

The shift means a deep, unequivocal setting the former ways down, or setting them aside. This functions similar to taking off an accessory that once fascinated us but now is no longer fashionable, or taking the trash to the curb instead of storing it in the closet.

See that releasing old habits and stored emotions, or breaking an addictive loop of a repetitive belief, or emptying the "personal me," is not something that we "have to do"... like running after our dog with a little bag when he squats in the neighbor's yard.

See this releasing, this emptying, as something we "get" to do, like smelling the sweet fragrance of a plumeria flower or floating over the ocean waves in an amber-rose, golden sunset.

Vital, spacious beauty Is.

Be that space where the miracle happens.

Be that Spirit Presence.

See: I already AM Spirit Self.

Be: The Quieting.

Stillpoint of Stillness Is; I Am That.

The Quieting Spirit aware of the Quieting Spirit.

Only this *emptying* into the ocean of Divine Love is the permanent answer. Emotional traumas and physical or emotional violence so deeply imprint us with defeat, worthlessness, rejection, and isolation, that nothing short of deep spiritual transformation will ever dissolve the pain and suffering.

The passage of time will not heal this. Psychology will not heal this. External changes will not heal this.

Only an authentic, deep, spiritual surrender into the ineffable, heals this.

Being alive as *Spirit Life* heals this by revealing *Presence Itself* as all that is present— in the *eternal, liberating, lasting way*.

All suffering is existential suffering.

This means that the existential sense of separation from that which created us arises as primal agony, stress sensations, and a core root of unhappiness.

It is not possible to feel separate from our Creator—and be truly happy. What passes off for modern day happiness is "seeking pleasure" and "avoiding pain."

Trauma occurs at the level of the psyche, soma (body), personality, and circumstances, which is this world of five senses and three dimensions. In the higher dimensional, high Spirit sense, these imprints do not occur.

And when alive as that Spirit Essence, the dense, misaligned thoughts, feelings, and imprints soften, flow, fade, and evaporate.

The realities of the golden world, of the *Light of Ahavah Presence*, shine brighter and brighter within and around the whole being, until remembrance dawns as *I Am That*.

Still… That.

The dark shadows of violence, trauma, fear, and pain, having within them even the tiniest spark of *Presence,* exist in reality as the totality of that Spirit Essence. Allow that tiny spark to ignite, illumine, and blaze brighter and brighter until it burns away all seeming shadows, forever.

Violence is weakness and it must "yield" to the *Light.* Darkness has no independent existence of its own.

Tenderness, as Light, exists as supreme strength. It ever uplifts, nourishes, nurtures, blesses.

In meekness, *reverence* the intimate, *Divine Tenderness* of the Light.

The Emptiness.

The Quieting.

Father Ahavah!

Experiential Application:
The Eternal Power of The Quieting

Realize that truth is simple and does not require complex steps.

These experiential applications offer remembrance triggers of what you naturally, simply already exist as, as the ground of being.

These flowing contemplations support in quieting the mind, the neurological system, and the emotions, to directly experience the *Spirit Life*.

As you read each phrase or two, pause, close your eyes, and relax into its experience.

This is not about learning or figuring out; it is about relaxing, emptying, releasing, un-conditioning.

These experiential practices support spacious, direct experience of *Eternal Spirit Presence, the Quieting*.

Father Ahavah Contemplative Prayer

- Notice if your neck, face or head feels warm or hot, as if there may be rising emotion or a "hot brain" that has a charge to the thoughts
- If so you may wish to place a cool damp washcloth on your forehead and/or top of head, and/or back of neck
- Find a comfortable position, sitting up, or reclining slightly back
- Allow slow deep full breaths, through the nose
- Allow shoulders to relax and the jaw and face to feel softer and softer
- Breathe in several seconds on the inhale and several seconds on the exhale, relaxing more with each exhale
- Have awareness of a slow, deep, circular breath, with no pauses
- Feel the breath... relax... allow the thoughts of the mind to slow down
- Slow thoughts by having *no interest* in them
- Having no interest in the thoughts... have interest in feeling the breath
- Have soft interest in releasing places of physical tension and contraction
- Scan the body for those places one by one, and relax and release them
- Have awareness of those places going soft, as if they are merging to the surrounding space, which you "see" or

"feel" as being love, being light *Presence*... take a couple of moments for this

- Relax the tiny muscles around the eyes, as if releasing to the space the feeling of anything you ever saw that you did not wish to see
- Release any tension or pressure or energetic contraction around the eyes or face, releasing the feeling of anything you wished to see and but that you did not see
- Place your left hand over your navel and right hand over your throat, and place tip of tongue on roof of mouth... relax and continue to breathe deeply, have awareness of the naturalness of "speaking from the depths, from the heart", and "it is safe to express"
- Feel ease and peace; feel the naturalness of self-honor
- Place your left hand over your eyes and eyebrows, the right hand over the crown of your head (top back area of head), keep tongue on roof of mouth, breathe deeply and slowly through nose for several breaths
- Rest your hands over your ears and temples, tongue tip on roof of mouth, and breathe, twice as long on the exhale (if you comfortably can) for several breaths... feel comfort... release sadness or any emotion that arises
- With hands facing inward, fingertips touching, rest your hands beneath your belly, cradling them around your lower abdomen... rest and relax for several breaths
- Move right hand over to center of lower abdomen and left hand to the correlating area behind your back (lower back), breathe several full deep breaths and relax... feel supported

- Place your left hand at center of front torso, at top of abdomen, and place right hand over left, breathe and relax into a nurturing feeling for several breaths… feel the natural flow of effortless power and grace
- Place your left hand over the center of your chest and the right hand over the left, keep tip of tongue on roof of the mouth, breathe deeply and contemplate *"I Exist as Spirit Presence, Eternally Safe"* (have an awareness of *Spirit* as all safe, with no opposite condition to safe)
- As best you can, in this moment allow the mind to quiet, not resisting thoughts, yet not interested in them or even noticing them
- As emotions are felt and released, and thoughts pass by without attention, the mind grows more and more quiet
- As best you can in this moment, let go of any worry, concern, or attention to persons, situations, events
- Simply *Softly Be*
- Keep your hands in one of those above positions you feel the most drawn toward, or simply relax them at your sides
- Be as, rest as, fall back into, the *Natural Immensity of Spirit Life*
- Feel that *Life* as *Safe*, as so safe there is no opposite to safe, and deeply rest
- Rest in and as *Spirit Aware of Spirit* (not giving attention in this moment to anything else)… take a moment to fall back into that, to contemplate that
- This is the true real *Secret: Spirit Presence One with God*, absorbing into, falling back into *Spirit Presence One With God*… aware of only *Spirit Presence One With God*, turning back again and again unto *Itself, not aware of anything else*

- *Father Ahavah Aware of Father Ahavah... feel this... absorbed into this... immerse in this... devoted to this... rest as this... exist as this*
- Imagine suffering, or violence has within its true essence, in the invisible "substratum" a spark of this same Spirit Light, this Spirit Presence... seemingly latent and absent... yet *Present*
- Similar to the eye of a storm, in any seeming storm of life, have an intention to see or feel *The Quieting* that is there at its core... *the Stillpoint of Peace* in the midst of chaos
- Rest into The *Quieting, the Peace Stillpoint* as if that is all that is there... take a moment for this
- Let go of analyzing or trying to think about it... open to directly feel and experience the still, quiet peace
- As you have attention, awareness, there, this comes alive
- No matter what the life situation looks like or feels like, release the fears of the past... or anxiety about the future... in this essence of Now, *Be The Quieting*
- *Ever feel for The Quieting*
- *The Quieting Aware of the Quieting*
- *Aware in this moment of nothing else... The Quieting... God Presence*
- *Have awareness of the Quieting, within all you look upon*
- Feel the love that is there beneath trespass, the oneness that is there beneath separation, the union that is there beneath indifference, the completion that is there beneath the appearance of lack or limitation

- It's as if from that invisible point you "expand" *The Quieting*, by "seeing" or "greeting" it, and it expands and expands until it fills all space
- Feel any residue of trauma grow softer and lighter (or it may first intensify, become unblocked or unlocked, and flow to its release)
- Abide as this safe nurturing, *The Quieting*, and allow any feelings of trauma or suffering to arise and merge-dissolve into *Original Tenderness*
- Remember the tiny spark of this Presence that is there, as if it again "grows" larger and larger and dissolves away anything other than this Spirit Presence
- Abide in the peace and happiness *of this changeless* safe, with no opposite to safe, and with no opposite to happiness or peace
- Allow nurturing, tender love, *Spirit Aware of Spirit*, to be more real, more true, more deep, more directly felt than suffering or trauma... or anything else
- Allow the thoughts, emotions, psyche, and neurological system to "feel" this, to directly immerse in this Light-Joy
- Ever more deeply "rest" as *Holy Spirit Aware of Holy Spirit*
- *The Quieting Aware of the Quieting*
- *Father Ahavah Aware of Father Ahavah*

Selah!

Chapter Seven

The Tap:

From Domination's Crushing To The Wings of The Free

Then

At age six, I debuted on the stage of the tap dance world. I had a big white smile on my eager face and big black bows on my shiny, patent leather black tap shoes. Creative mystic, terrazzo floor, and thrilling taps merged in natural harmony.

In spontaneous moments, an invisible inner dancer ignited, like an angel of unleashed freedom, flying across the dance floor. She led the way in each leaping second, leaving my little girl body to catch up somehow.

I loved the excitement of performing and seeing everyone's attentive smiles. And the costumes were shimmering silk and enchanting chiffon. I wondered if anyone else noticed the best part of the costumes: the invisible space around them that sparkled like pure seamless magic.

At age nine, I eagerly performed the solo at a senior assisted living facility. My costume was bright red sequins with snowy white fur along the neckline. (About a year ago I found that costume, and the fabric was stretchy enough that I shimmied into it and paraded around the house, to the dismay and jealous amusement of my weight-conscious friends).

I formed a close bond with Debbie, my tap dance teacher. I offered my innocence, devotion, bravery, and determinedness, and she offered that certain light in the eye and rushing proudness on the face that says, "Yes, she just did that," and "that's my girl."

I had no idea of the depth and significance of that bond, how hungry I was for *someone* to be proud of me, until it was stolen from me. At first she was the pretty face and encouraging voice once a week. As years went on, she became one of the most stable, consistent, relationships in my life.

That made her invaluable.

Weekly dance lessons somehow survived the destabilizing family dynamics and constant moving, until I went to live with my father at age eleven.

Mom no longer drove me to tap lessons; Dad did. The drives to and from grew increasingly stressful. I could feel his "trapped into this" resistance.

Usually he didn't show up until after class ended.

One night, I was so excited; I could not wait to tell him that my tap dance teacher had given me surprising and wonderful news. She expressed her delight at my talent and acknowledged me as one of her top students. She wished to work with me privately, one on one.

"And, Dad, you won't believe this... she wants me to do more stage performances and even duet performances *with her!"*

This breakthrough—this new level of attentive interaction with her—offered sorely needed validation for me. It created a positive upward focus and a vital opportunity to find a "family" feeling that felt safe and untroubled.

As we drove home, I bubbled over with enthusiasm. A despondent aching longing now had a potential fulfillment. I appealed to him with the hopeful thrill of a child, hoping against hope for some small good fortune.

My heart sank when Dad's face hardened into aggravation. He sharply pointed out, "private lessons are more expensive." I winced at his scoffing: "That's ridiculous, you're not that good of a dancer."

I offered him the heart of the daughter: trusting, open-hearted, wishing to bring him joy. He withdrew in that rigid head space that shuts off the flow of love and joy, the way a blocked artery shuts off oxygen flow to the heart.

I weakly mustered up, *"But Dad,* she thinks I am special, and I'll have more time *with her."*

I tried to mask the little telltale quiver in my voice with a show of inflated assurance, even as I felt that sinking sensation. I knew I was losing ground.

I tried not to cower as the heat mounted. He irritably pointed out the difference in cost and my shortcomings as a dancer.

My confidence melted fast, but I tried, "I could babysit for the extra; I can earn the extra to pay for it."

No reply.

"Please Dad."

No reply.

"I will perform at charities and help people."

No reply.

He kept driving, staring straight ahead.

I stared straight ahead, forcing back the tears and sitting up straighter.

My heart beat faster, my mind wildly conjured things to say. Sadness welled up, choking my throat. Why was everything a battle? Why couldn't he just *love me*?

I couldn't prevent the tearfulness from seeping into my words, as they quivered out, "*She said I am really, really good.*"

His terse reply cut me. "I've seen you dance. You are not any better than anyone else. The other girls in class are just as good or better. *You are not that great! No private lessons. In fact, you don't need to go anymore at all!*"

Crushed.

True communication joins. This did not offer communication. This exemplified a power struggle.

Far beyond the smoke screen of a few dollars a month, his withholding of the father's heart, his refusal to offer the warming fires of compassion and encouragement, seared my hopes.

My vulnerability did not stand a fighting chance against this unyielding opponent. This masculine "force" came to oppose. When this fatherly wall perceived a challenge, *it would crush its opponent.*

I ached… I deeply longed to be the apple of his eye, to see him beam at the sight of me, just because I was "his."

In that moment, *I wasn't his daughter.* I was nothing special. I was nothing.

I held my whole chest and body tight, in an effort not to cry.

And then I collapsed in total defeat and my voice choked through the tears, "Ok! I just won't ever go at all again!"

The closed-hearted reply came: "Fine."

And that was the end of that.

There was never a circling back with "Daughter, I thought about it, and that was too hard on you. You could babysit for the extra; I won't see you quit like this." Or "I know what this means to you, let's work it out." Much less a loving response: "You are a wonderful dancer, and let's make this happen together, I would love to see your new performances and how you make people smile."

I never tap danced again.

More significantly, the father wound deepened and the dance in my heart died a little more.

These repetitive defeats, progressively singed my confidence that I could speak my truth, open my heart, and be heard and honored. Over time, the innate luminosity of my voice in the world burned to gray ash.

My dance lessons ended, and the connection with my dance teacher was abruptly and forever severed. I never saw or spoke to Debbie again.

The sorrowful resentment toward my father grew. Yet I feared that resentment, and submerged it until it turned into despair, dark and heavy as molasses.

At the time, I didn't think the word "cruel." I felt powerless, worthless, depressed.

Helplessness-anger.

I felt waves of little shocks to my neurological and emotional systems. Precious things were being destroyed—my heart, my longing for father bond, another close relationship —and all I could do was watch, and bottle up the hurt inside.

The knot in the pit of my stomach solidified; the constriction in my throat pulled in tighter, and the heat rose and fired up the spinning thoughts.

He doesn't care. I want a father! Nothing I say matters. I miss my dance teacher. How come I don't live with Mom? I want to dance. When can I move out? Oh yeah, eighteen. I wish I were eighteen. I wish I wasn't here at all. How come he doesn't love me? He's the one I need things from but when I go to him he hurts me. There is no one... no one!

The emotional pressure felt tumultuous, like some ancient collective trespass rising up. Fear of—and disrespect of—the feminine. A negation of the sacred. An impasse.

A child feeling the global ancient pain.

The wall.

It was the hitting of the ancient wall.

Aching for a loving embrace, I was beating my young head and vulnerable heart against an unyielding wall.

It is not just hitting the wall that creates despair.

It is the *repetitive hitting of the unrelenting wall* that creates the despair.

I realized much later I wasn't just hitting the wall of my dad. I wasn't just hitting the wall of my feelings. I hit the wall of collective unconscious, of collective selfishness. I hit the wall of feeling separate from *God Presence.*

And those walls turned to mazes inside; inner obstacles of self-sabotage, deep pain and stored emotions.

Dad stooped to lower levels of obstruction, until he broke me and I cried out, "I'll never go again." And then he said "Fine." He had triumphed.

He controlled the situation with his daughter to avoid the inconvenience of driving and nine extra dollars a month. And he controlled my request for support and nurturing, by making it so painful that I avoided asking.

He won.

But he lost.

He lost my love, my respect, and my devotion. And he lost the joy of a true relationship by settling for this fake love.

He lost the connection to *his* feminine creativity, to *his* masculine strength, to the *Divine Presence* that is the Reality of "him." He lost connection to the *Love* he exists as in *Reality*.

He did not inquire of himself, *"Why do I feel anger about her dancing?"*

There would have been nothing "wrong" with any feeling that arose in him. Love is not lost because a feeling arises.

Love was lost because he did not deeply "sit with" and unwind those feelings. And he did not call himself to model love, communication, or solidarity.

Love was lost because he felt separate from God, the *Heart of Father God*.

Rather than creating with me, he competed with me.

And he nearly always won.

And when he won he lost.

We both did.

Now

The moment I saw the historical estate, I recognized it as the perfect reflection of my envisioned home and spiritual retreat. Some people call it spectacular—like a storybook paradise. Another jokingly refers to it as "the mansion of Jackie O."

To me, it is sacred.

To me, it is *Home.*

I feel a deep and exquisite bond to the land, as with no other space on earth.

And yet I'm aware that *Home is God Spirit,* and after all, this is just a place, a space.

From the beginning of my time living here, there arose a natural bond with the trees, the animals, the ancestors, and the very earth. I sit with my back against the welcoming and majestic oak trees. I intimately *know* the animals—regal and protective ospreys, curious and playful squirrels, rambunctious and adorable raccoons.

Flashes of ancient, sacred rituals and prayer gatherings arise on the mounds of the land.

Sitting with the living trees, I experience Self and the property as *Light*. The land opens to call forth and receive restoration and christening.

A spiritual elder visited and said, "It is glorious to see you take this land back." He paused, looked pleasantly surprised, and asked himself, *Why did I say "take this land back?"* And then he saw the same visions I had seen.

Something about moving to this homeland, being restored to this *spirit land,* sparked fiery resurrections; flaming torches of insights alighted and blazed like a great bonfire of destiny.

One of those restorations ignited a few weeks after setting my feet on the property; I had a sudden urge to tap dance.

I had not thought of tap dancing in years.

I had no teacher, studio, or shoes. Yet, I could feel the moves within me.

I found the name of a local teacher and left her a voicemail.

As I was pulling into the parking lot of Michael's Crafts, the phone rang. A voice said, "Hi, I'm Christy. I'm calling about your tap lesson."

Suddenly the decades-old conversation with Dad flashed through me. My vocal cords locked up. I felt the pain of the father-wound rise and yet instantly dissolve in *Father Ahavah,* Divine Father Love.

"Hello?... Hello, are you there?"

"Yes. I tapped for years as a child. I am an adult now, calling for a private lesson."

"Do you have your shoes?"

I felt surprised; I had no idea where they were. Did someone throw them away?

"Hello?"

"Yes, I'm here. No, no tap shoes."

"What size are you?"

"Seven."

"Ok, I have an old pair."

"Thanks, I'll use yours."

"When do you want to come?"

"Tomorrow?"

"Two o'clock tomorrow!"

I hung up the phone and sat in the parking lot, very, very still. I softly welcomed a subtle, hidden layer of trauma feelings that surfaced and dissolved into the heart space of *Love*. Some missing piece of the puzzle was about to fill in. In all the immensity of *Spirit Presence*, what meaning could tap dancing have?

That night, I pulled out my photo albums and books, searching for childhood photos.

I found my adult photos instead... rabbit after rabbit—bunnies I had rescued and raised. Photos of my favorite themes: temples, churches, oceans, trees, rabbits.

I smiled at photos of Israel near Galilee, where Jesus spoke the beatitudes, the sermon on the mount. *Blessed are the pure in heart, for they shall see God (Matthew 5:8)*. Photos emerged of the green and gentle Dead Sea, and the golden temples of the holy city, Safed. And I saw again the deep blue oceans of Montserrat, as I embraced a sea of children that I served in the mission work there.

Looking back I felt *Father God Love,* beaming through in all of these places. This *Love* shone like a lighthouse of salvation's redemption, calling the suffering, unfathered ones home to this *Love.*

Like the tiny thrill of finding lost keys, I smiled to discover a childhood tap photo. The picture popped with color: a bright white and kelly green polka-dot costume, fishnet tights, hat in hand, head tilted, big smile, tap shoes. Then another photo fell out of the stack to land face up on the floor. I reached down to retrieve my picture of the red-sequins costume, trimmed with white fur. And the next find: age six—baby skin, big eyes, golden hair, looking tiny and eager in a bright orange and black chiffon costume.

The next day I walked into the studio in causeless happiness and detached equanimity. An occasional hot tear, making its way down my cheek, felt like a gentle washing away of some secret chard that had finally loosened up and let go.

I tossed the little photo book on the table and said, "Here is my portfolio." Christy grinned at the childhood photos. She looked at me intently, with curiosity.

Walking across the floor in tap shoes, I felt animation returning as my body said "yes."

We started off slowly, and after a few moments she said, "You're not a beginner; let's try intermediate." I felt relieved and the lesson began to flow faster.

She began to comment, "Wow, you are picking this up really fast… let me get my other sound track… goodness, you really remember after all these years!"

I felt joy, and yet also felt caged.

Finally I said, "I would like to do the wings."

She said "Wings?!"

I steadily replied, "Yes."

"Oh no! Wings are beyond advanced, They're at the "tricks" level of dance. You can't do that."

I quietly looked at her, telepathically emanating "wings!"

Father memories flashed. I surrendered softly, into the reality *"I Exist As, I Am Spirit, One with The Eternal Father Love."* That laser beam of remembrance calmed the trembling remnants of grief from loss of fatherly love. The felt *Presence* of simple, natural *Sacredness* washed away the leftover fragments of the daughter's empty ache of longing for masculine nurturing and protection. Greater calmness arose.

Being an aware, responsive being, Christy stopped, looked at me and said, "Later you can show me your wings."

I smiled as she responded to my holding the space of calm knowing.

The impassioned energized fluidity of wings... something in me was bursting for that pivotal moment.

The time finally came.

She insisted I hold the bar. I stood and held the bar.

I was not going keep holding the bar, no matter what she said. That would not factor into the equation.

Then calmly, yet somehow wildly, I ditched the bar and glided to the center of the floor, hands free, and passionately executed perfect wings, wings, wings.

A part of my *power* flew back into my being. And after all the wings, breathless and laughing, I jumped in the air and let out a yell like some kind of tribal victory chant.

Christy watched attentively. She had that delighted "she's mine... she's my student!" look on her face. She laughed until she nearly cried in amazed joy.

I realized that all of these years, the only thing stopping me from tap dancing was the invisible lack of permission, the unconscious loss of sovereignty.

The Reality of Presence had moved "me" on the dance floor. And I could feel something else moving through me, something *other* — the whole free, ecstatic universe.

That did not surprise me.

What surprised me was how the physical body was longing for this movement, this expression that had been "stolen" from it, to be returned.

The body knows. It remembers. And in the dancing, something that had been lost was restored. I noticed that the body even walked a little taller, and the muscles and legs felt like they had in youth.

We are not the body. Yet the body, released of contractions and memory, resonates as *Spirit Light*.

Limitations are more imaginary than we realize. No matter what seems "lost" or "stolen," none of that has reality or true power.

Our lost will, lost choices, lost voice, can never really be *lost*. Redemption of all power exists here now, forever.

We are tricked into thinking our wings are clipped.

And we sit, at ground level. Unaware, we may overlook or forget things for years, believing that we are incapable of flight because of an old story that we innocently created.

When we lose something by trauma, often it disappears from our "range of perceived choices."

We no longer even think of an original vision, or have the courage to move toward our limitless way of being. When we lose confidence or feel defeated in our attempt at something, we may shut down to the point that it no longer even exists in our field of possibilities.

At times, the defeat is so severe and crushing that we have an aversion or avoidance to that very thing which actually reflects our highest fulfillment—the perfect expression of living, beyond our wildest imagination.

Yet *all the while,* our wings alight golden, vast, infinite, and limitless, and we may soar above anything, into heaven's way of astounding fulfillment.

Listen for the stirrings of Spirit.

Awaken as the aliveness of *limitless Spirit*. Listen to and follow the whisperings of how *It* wishes to express. Follow *Spirit Life* as "your individualized expression."

Now, I see that I could have babysat for the money, taken the city bus, and continued tap dancing. I could have continued to nurture the bond with my teacher, who was such a stable point of relationship. But the internal crushing was so severe that I did not perceive those possibilities. I shut down, my will weakened and paralyzed.

Now, there is an awareness of *Reality* as *Limitless Presence*. The limiting beliefs and emotional storage have released, with no sense of victimhood.

Our inheritance, our birthright, is the ability to dance boundlessly through life—through the galaxies as *Living Light*. It is our natural direct experience, if we can only realize it. In my life, those glimpses of limitlessness have gained a momentum of fluidity and frequency.

Open your heart, remember *Home,* and rest as that *Spirit Presence, that Infinite Love*. Behold that Presence animate, in creative form.

Behold *It* form your life experience as freedom, benevolence, and astounding grace.

Know Father Ahavah as the bestower of your golden wings.

Fly free with your *infinite wings.*

Experiential Application:

The Glory of the Wings

The Divine Papa Tenderness That Births The Limitless

Allow space between the phrases to close your eyes, and rest in the feeling and essence of the message, before opening eyes to read the next phrase.

These are not complex practices or complicated steps. The phrases simply lovingly guide you *Home*. They support remembrance of the causeless happiness you already exist as, in the spiritual heart.

Keep it simple; remember, the reality of freedom is already here this instant.

- Allow yourself to settle into a comfortable position
- Rest and relax into full, deep, slow breaths
- Allow the breath to be circular, full, deep... in and out of the nose
- Take at least several seconds for the inhale and for the exhale, without pauses between the inhale and exhale
- Allow a couple of moments for this circular relaxed breath that has no pauses at the top of the inhale or the bottom of the exhale
- Allow the forehead muscles to relax

- Soften the face and allow the head to feel more expanded and light
- Relax the shoulders, and the muscles along the spine
- Allow the whole body to relax
- Softly contemplate: *"I exist as Spirit, as One With God, as Limitless, as Free"*... pause and contemplate the phrase for a few moments *rest*
- Gently think of the phrase, and then relax and fall back into *Spirit Presence*
- Remember, *"I Exist as Spirit, One with God, Limitless"*... and release thought of this world... releasing worry, concern or thought of persons, relationships, the body, finances, work, contribution
- Have an awareness of having huge "wings" (capacity to reflect the glory of Spirit Life)
- With compassion, one with Divine Love, meet the emotional content of feeling crushed or defeated
- Divine Love dissolves this pain... feel this... as best you can... rest in the heart
- Allow an emptying of memories, past, beliefs, thoughts, emotional contraction around feeling crushed by the masculine (or anyone or anything)
- Yet, stay more aware of *Spirit Presence* than the emotions or memories—this is a huge key
- Be Spirit Presence, above and beyond emotions and beliefs
- Allow any anger, and the underlying sadness and grief to gently unlayer, in the full *Light* of the *Tenderness of Divine Grace*

- Allow any emotions to surface from the pain of feeling doubted, forgotten, not the apple of the eye of the Father's Heart
- See these emotions as simply sensations... not complex named emotions... simple unnamed story-less sensations
- Contemplate: *"I Am the Spirit Love aware of the emotions, that upon which emotions rise and fall"*
- Allow any remaining longings for the masculine love to surface and be welcomed into love
- Release this *longing-ness... allow its sensation to be nameless... and to soften and fade*
- Open to deeply, intimately feel the *Love of the Father*, the *Heart of the Spirit Father*
- *Realize this Father Ahavah, Divine Father Love as an Unconditional Principle,* now here "for you", available in you, as you...
- Contemplate the *Divine Masculine God Presence*, closer than the breath, within you, embracing you
- Open to the *One Presence, One Completion*, of both masculine and feminine with nothing missing or withheld, realize that *God is Light, and Light* is beyond gender
- Realize: *"I am Spirit, beyond gender, yet the completion of masculine and feminine as One;* take a moment to rest and contemplate this balance, this peace...
- Realize: *"I already am Spirit Self-Completion"...* rest in this for a moment...
- Rest in and feel this completion... open to remember being it...

- Continue to allow emotions that arise in this moment, or over the coming times, to be welcomed into Love, and dissolved into peace
- No need to try to dissolve an emotion... refrain from trying to dissolve it
- Simply see it is there and leave it be, without suppressing it, nor giving it power to sustain or maintain itself...
- See former patterns, beliefs, emotions as "this is leaving"... dissolving... fading... *trust in that*
- Welcome the totality of the belief-emotion-sensations, and softly, spaciously "sit with it" without moving into thoughts, blame, persons, or stories
- Right there within the contracted emotions is the whole expanse of *Spirit Love, Limitlessness, Spacious Golden Wings*
- Allow the *Spirit Wings Presence* to grow so potent that it envelops all thought, feeling, memory, situations into the boundless *Presence*
- See that nothing and no one dims that brilliance
- Allow the *Heart of Father God* to feel so close, as an intimate communion and feel *Father Grace and Father Blessings* shine upon you, already present within you
- Feel as a beloved daughter (or son) of the *Creator, Abba Father, the Divine Papa of all Light and Eternal Love*
- *Open to—in a subtle way or a profoundly riveting way— experience Eternal Papa's* attentive adoring gaze of *Love* upon you
- ***Sit with that, as if that were the only observation you exist under—Father Ahavah adoration!***

- *Notice how you feel, who you are, under the gaze of this Divine Papa, Father Ahavah!*
- *Feel the redemption of knowing self as sacred, as limitless wings, as loved, as love...*
- *Have awareness of Oneness with and as Eternal Papa, Father Ahavah*
- *Yet there are not "two," just like the ocean and the ocean wave are one... you are one with this* Eternal Father Love, *alive as the Heart of this Eternal Father Love*
- Realize the *Divine Presence* is not inaccessible to you, not sought or earned; and there is nothing to prove and nothing withheld
- It is accessible to you this instant... is closer than the breath, the *Home Reality* of *Divine Love* you already exist as
- *Still Home*
- No wall exists in *this Divine Papa Love*
- Father Ahavah Presence is *so accessible to you, you are enveloped into it, adored by it, created As It*
- In the *Heart of Father God,* as Divine Father Love, *Ahavah's Love Gaze* lights you up, revealing *You as the Light*
- See that at some level, all limitations are imposed imaginary conditioning, not solid, or unyielding walls
- They are similar to chalk marks on a childhood sidewalk that you simply step beyond, forever release, and fly free from with golden wings
- Realize: "Awakened in the Light of Divine Papa's adoring gaze, I am wings of glory, limitless and free"
- *Father Ahavah Wings*
- *I Am the Light!*

Selah!

Chapter Eight

The Vulnerability

From The Vulnerable One To The Feminine As Light & Peace

Then

He was 28; I was 13.

I assumed that when Dave visited us or invited me to go places with him, that my father would be present also.

Over time, it stopped working out that way.

Initially I found it mildly odd to spend time alone with Dave. He was my *father's* friend.

I queried: "How come Dad isn't coming with us to Disney World?" "Are just the two of us spending the day at the water slide?" Was Dave a babysitter, a friend, a kind of brother, a stand-in father? I wasn't quite sure.

My elders sent me off with him, so I accepted it. I felt a flicker of hope of this evolving into a stable relationship with a protective caretaker. I surmised, *Well, Dad is with his girlfriend, Mom is with this new person, my brother is always out with his friends, so I guess I am "with Dave."* Other people were now special to them, and being "with Dave" meant that I was special to Dave.

I thought of him as my friend or elder… the person I did things with when other people were busy. He offered a refuge from the discordance at home, and this formed a natural bond between us.

I longed to feel welcomed, to truly belong… *somewhere… with someone.*

At middle school craft class I etched flowers in a leather key chain for him. I listened to his radio show at 6:00 in the morning and felt a special connection when he intentionally played my favorite songs. I joined the cheers of the crowd from the stadium, at Dave's radio station baseball games. My father played on the team too. And they made me tag along to the sports bar afterward.

I felt a little bit like the apple of this man's eye, and that gained my trust. His appreciation for what he deemed my rare and beautiful qualities—my intuition, candor, innocence, depth, and quick wit—fit like a key into the lock of my longing for significance.

I remained naive as to the way my unmet emotional needs rendered me a sitting duck—or young swan of vulnerable loveliness—for insincere predators. As a child-woman, my tender feminine feelings left me an open target for a man with hidden motives.

Dave fit the stereotype of tall, dark and handsome. His morning radio show, delivered in his rich, deep voice, brought him acclaim. He was six foot, successful, and confident. I was little, honey eyed, and forgotten by my family.

He shone like a star at planning our amusements—Disney World, Busch Gardens, water slides, the zoo, movies, skiing, swimming, playing, and laughing. He failed miserably at food—I endured his rubbery bologna sandwiches just to receive his smile.

However, water-skiing outings revealed a creepy, emotionless side of him. He skied on *forever*, with a blank stare on his face. I watched from the back of the boat, alternating between feeling bored and feeling rattled. I sent telepathic messages like, *Geez, just drop the ropes and let me go out there and do some trick skiing, or you could at least cross the wake and smile a little*. I waved and grinned at him, but he just looked serious and disconnected. When *I* skied, *I connected* with the splashing azure deep water, the slick wooden ski, the tree-lined land caressing the shoreline, and the force of wild wind whipping my long hair.

After awhile, I noticed other aspects to Dave. I perceived his subtle craving for attention and the way he maneuvered himself as the focal point in social gatherings. Once, at the bar, a woman told well-received jokes. Suddenly, Dave interrupted and loudly told funny stories, slapping his thigh and laughing so hard at himself that everyone turned their attention to him. Even his sports car had a huge, noisy pipe on the side; it stuck out so far that it burned my leg one day when I climbed into the car.

However, when we were alone together, he put the focus on me in a fatherly or brotherly way, which made me feel quite special. This handsome, popular man paid attention *to me*. And I longed to *really belong* to *someone*.

I didn't *really belong* to my family anymore. My chest ached to be soothed by the warm, affectionate knowing that it *really mattered* to *someone* that I existed.

For years before the Dave friendship, the belief that no one cared if I *was there* or *was not there* seeped into my innermost heart, eroding my esteem with rusty demoralization. It welled up as a tarnished sadness, an alloyed sorrow that stored up in my cells and psyche. It multiplied like a virus, weakening my immunity to stress and my ability to spring back from life's challenges.

Dave had a way of letting me know that it mattered if I was there, and mattered if I was not there. Once I walked up with overall blue-jean shorts and pigtails, and petite as I was, he smiled and proudly said, "The Big A," affirming and celebrating *me*.

I later discovered him as a Big A ____ in a very different sort of way. Not in ultimate reality, since all beings share the sacred seed of Divine Life. However, in the patterns of his personality character—in his choices to devolve and harm—he shirked accountability for violating innocence.

At times he encouraged me to miss a day at school and spend time with him. I felt safer and more familiar with him than at my third school in three years.

One evening, at his bachelor pad, I asked what time he planned to drive me home. He casually inquired as to the whereabouts of my father. I answered that he had gone out for the night.

Then he said something he had not ever said before. He slyly replied, "The cat's out of the bag."

My skin pricked and my stomach felt uneasy. His expression didn't look right and that sounded odd. But he was my best friend in the whole world.

He tried to kiss me, and slid his tongue into my mouth. He unzipped his pants, exposing himself, and pushed my head down. I recoiled and pushed him away.

Sick with nausea, I ran and locked myself in the bathroom. My world unraveled and destabilized. He had been friend, my only real one and I needed his protection. I couldn't bear another loss.

I felt overwhelmed with confusion and wished to get away. The bond of trust crumbled.

I said, "I want to go home," and he took me home.

Dealing with this alone, the stress mounted. I had looked up to him, and he ripped the trust out from under me. I sat alone shaking, thirteen and naively confused. Did he plan to marry me one day when I grew up? Should I hold a boundary until we are married, or should I never see my one friend again?

For the first time in my life, I started to *pace*.

I sat, hurled into *a new* initiation into pain, which I lacked the developmental skills to handle. I had no elders or guides to turn to for wisdom or safe passage.

After that, I spent less time with him and avoided going to his place. Confused and distressed, I spent more time alone. Eventually I shut down and withdrew completely.

One day, from my upstairs window, I heard the loud car pipes screaming for attention, as he drove up to visit my father. Without thinking, I grabbed the leather key chain I'd made for him and flew downstairs and out to the parking lot. I had an icky sense of knowing who he *really* was: the man who had tainted my innocence. Why couldn't he just treat me *kindly and decently?*

He walked toward me, saying, "I love you." That surprised me. I threw the leather gift at him and cried out, "That's not love… you ruined everything!" And then hot salty tears streaked my face as I choked out, "You were all I had, my only real friend."

I ran upstairs sobbing, feeling the unrecoverable betrayal. He was the only person that had a special fondness for me. I wanted a real relationship so badly, but not like that—not without trust, not being violated, not feeling nasty.

No one.

I told my father. He would be angry at Dave, maybe never speak to him again.

All the adults arranged for me to spend time with him. I had never done anything "wrong" with Dave; in fact, I stopped his advances. I chose emotional isolation rather than let him touch me.

But then I saw the look on Dad's face.

My father entered my room and pulled up a chair directly across from me. His words stung, like punishing lashes on my face. "You are so stupid! Dave has dated ten girls since I've known him, and his girlfriend Janet from up north is moving here. He didn't kiss you, you are lying! What would he want with you? Or if he did it must be your fault! You will be punished!"

His angry tone and cynical expression hurt more than his words. In that critical moment, I needed the reparation of a father's protection—not the disowned guilt of a male oppressor who distorted me into "the badness."

I was the badness.

It was his golden moment as my father to offer masculine protection and restore my feeling of goodness and innocence. Instead he tossed in his own log to the fires of exploitation.

My cheeks burned red with humiliation.

I felt like he'd punched me in the stomach, deflating my power. My father hurled more blame missiles like poisoned darts. Even though I knew I did not deserve them, these emotional carcinogens slipped into my heart, like a cancer eating away my self-esteem. I struggled for composure, suppressing the silent hysteria inside. *The freeze.*

For some twisted reason, my father protected the perpetrator and punished the innocent one. He scapegoated me for something I had never done, and in that crucial moment, I felt the sinking awareness: "I am not *his daughter.*"

He extended his loyalty to a pedophile.

This went beyond being too easy on an unknown pedophile with a faceless victim, which is bad enough— it rings with an unconscionable tone. He stood in allegiance to, and retained friendship with the man who traumatized *his young daughter.* He too casually passed his child off to someone who turned out as a narcissistic sex offender, and then evaded accountability and restoration.

I sat there, shaking in stunned disbelief, assessing the double betrayal of the two most influential men in my life. This out-of-order insanity confused me more than someone spinning me round and round in a swivel chair, until I was too dizzy to retain balance. I didn't know or use the words "scapegoat" or "pedophile." I just knew something felt sickening and loathsome.

I welled up with a stinging *false* shame. Though I knew I hadn't done anything wrong, after my father's tirade I felt *I was* the wrongness... *the badness*. But how could that be? So often I recognized my innocence. Reality twirled and twisted; why was my innocence being made ugly?

I had lost my family. I had lost my mom. I lost my tap dance teacher. I lost school after school as we moved, and I lost all the friends in those schools. I lost my sense of worth and esteem, and no longer felt safe in the world or even in my house. And now Dave.

I turned myself inside out to make sense of life, relationships and the world. I tried to hold it all together like a juggling clown, as more and more balls were thrown at her. I missed more and more school. I pulled the covers over my head, wishing I could stay in bed all day. Eventually, at times I did just that.

I wanted to die. There was nowhere to go, no one to talk to, no safe harbor that I could trust. I felt so fragile, so *vulnerable*.

My tender feelings were crushed so often that I was *becoming the crushing*, rather than the creative, dancing, spirit child I could have been.

It was only a few months later that my father delivered the severe blows to my head for being too "loud."

Then came the stronger wanting to die.

I thought of just sinking to the bottom of the sea and staying there.

Instead, I walked along the ocean for long hours.

One day I rambled along the sugary sand beach on the Gulf of Mexico. Suddenly I had visions of crowds of people, like snippet flashes of the future. Over a period of days, more images arose, and I felt a sweet, innocent perfume of peace pervade my whole being. I felt *God Presence*, like an angelic, compassionate calm.

In these flashes, I spoke to crowds of people, overflowing with gentle joy and profound peace. Yet, it wasn't "me." A profound ineffable depth of the most pure holy compassion imaginable spoke through me. I felt the stunning beauty of this deep compassion of the *Heart of Father God*.

The people who were suffering could feel God Presence within them, and were healed, in every way—in emotions, relationships, affluence, harmony, kindness. And when I sat with them, in reverence of this *Grand Glorious Presence*, they felt that same *Presence*. And I saw they *were* one with a spark of this *Presence* in Reality.

One day the visions came and I *directly experienced the pure, holy Light of God*. And the people in my life—beneath or beyond personalities—were this same *God-feeling* Light. And I knew that where me—the girl—is, *God Is,* and where all these other people are, *God Is.*

And this God was *kind,* and *friendly,* and *welcoming.* It was *Home.*

It was pure, holy, and it would never leave. *I was unified with It and It was the true essence of me.*

And I sensed that when the people in my vision were happy, what they really felt was this union in God Light, under all the "human stuff" that falls apart. And when they were critical and punishing, beneath that they were *still* this God Light, but they had just forgotten. And when they forgot that they were this loving Light, it hurt too much to bear, and so they, in turn, did things that hurt too much to bear.

The desire to die lifted. I knew God Spirit as Life. Even after the visions stopped, this deep *Love* and *Peace within remained.*

It was so subtle. As I let all else drop away to be this subtle peace, it grew more and more potent. *I blossomed under the gaze of God, not people.* It arose as immaculate joy; safe beyond imagination.

And under this safe gaze I was not the shameful badness. I never had been. I existed as one with Original Innocence and could only be that. And that was the true core of everyone.

That knowing lifted my heart and secretly carried me along in life, for long periods of time.

Still though, as daily life encroached and relationship hurts flared, that *Reality faded* and seemed so far away again. Painful situations and inner suffering overwhelmed me again; they felt more real than the subtle peace.

I longed to feel the peace of *God Presence* ceaselessly.

One morning I woke up very early; it was still dark. I felt pulled to the ocean by something wise, grand and all-pervasive. My bare feet glided across the silky, naked sands of the Gulf of Mexico. I came alive; a magical, sacred feeling sent chills up my spine. I knew I was not alone, and this *Something* was calling me.

The blue-black ocean, illumined with shimmering moon dust, frolicked in welcoming magnificence. The frothy waves roared in swirls of rich salt and wet wind. The dancing ocean cascaded on the opal sands with a heart-satisfying majesty.

The soft moon smiled, and its diamond light rained down like silver stars tickling the ebony waves. I heard the pre-dawn's mysterious silent laughter, and breathed in sync with the serene waves rising and falling upon the mysterious depths that plunged down, deeper than deep.

The sky glowed silken, deep lavender-black, while soft fingers of amber-rose dawn crept up from the honeyed horizon, tenderly ushering in *Light*.

The dancing waves and soft sugary sand enlivened the soles of my feet. The ocean *and the Presence* serenely sashayed over my legs, fortifying my essential purpose to build a life foundation of devotion.

The Light unified me with the baptismal feel of the cleansing water. The dolphins, called by tones of love and wonder, spiraled up out of the water and swam along the shore in rhythm with my stride and the celestial beat of my awakening heart.

As I reached the dunes of Caladesi Island, the sun rose, like a golden ball of Original Light.

A gentle love arose in my heart, akin to a holy ceremony.

In that simple moment, something special flashed in my awareness and planted a seed.

A gentle, comforting, and powerful knowing dawned: *Your parents are not your real parents.*

I couldn't quite put it into any other words; I just knew it was true somehow.

God, this loving Divine Presence, was my *Parents*.

Mother God was my Mother and she would mother me and teach me the *Heart of the Mother*. And *Father God was my Father* and would show me the *Heart of the Father*.

At times that felt *so real*.

I knew it as Eternally Real.

At other times, everything of the sensory, phenomenal world felt more real.

Yet, these direct experiences of the Reality of the golden world—the sane world not of this world—kept me alive.

In those rare moments, I was The Sacred Aliveness.

When those rich oases arose, the pain and struggle washed away. In those sacred instants beyond the boundaries of time, I knew the reality of heaven right here, in the midst of the world's hollow sinkholes and the mirage of its hells.

I saw that the two "worlds" could both seem to be there. I didn't know how to make the True One—*the Reality, God is my parents, Light Is*—real all the time.

I did perceive that I would find out—and I was destined to speak to crowds of people about it when I grew up.

God is my Parents.

If I could really know that, then I could *only* be the offspring of God.

Now

Almost always now, the *Spirit Self, the kindness reality*, is more real than the hells of separation.

Sometimes, for a brief instant, the illusion of the hellish experiences feels more real. Then remembrance dawns that pain is simply arising from a contraction and a resistance. In opening the heart to the contraction, I perceive a spark of Light, of "love space" in the middle of the rising emotions. I behold that dot, that spark of love, expand as Light, and it swallows up the tightness of suffering like an alchemy of expansive peace.

Holy ineffable *Presence* gently pulses *tangibly* as the majestic ground of Self. The body—no longer being the receptacle of stored emotion, but being the *Presence* that emotions rise and fall within—feels truly lighter and more radiant.

The past often seems like the same essence as last night's dream; the characters, emotions and thoughts feel similar to a movie. Looking back on the past, even a moment ago, has a similar movie-like feel. Rather than seeming tangible, solid, real, at times it feels more temporal, changeable, fluid. In other words, the Reality is more rooted as *Presence, Spirit, God Light*, than in the changing, shifting scenes of life.

All of this rises and falls upon *Compassion Presence*.

As I child, the episode with Dave spiraled me into confusion on so many levels beyond my developmental age. I had no way to process, language or integrate it. A naïve thought like, *Am I going to marry him?* may not have occurred to a teen with cohesive family bonds and a strong reference point of healthy nurture and belonging. A child left too much alone in the deep heart places, too rejected by elders, sits emotionally unprotected—an easy target for a predator to take advantage of their youth, innocence, and trust.

Fortunately, I summoned the courage and awareness to listen to those nudges of "wrongness" and my body's stress signals when he made sexual advances.

The most pervasive cut—the repeating effects—spans beyond the original wound. The wound shatters the sense of self, stagnates in reservoirs of pain, and imprints us with *unyielding* sabotage patterns.

Though methods such as psychology, positive thinking, and introspective therapy offer tools of self-acceptance and improved relationships, none of them go deep enough to heal those deep wounds at our core. Only the deep union with/as *God Presence*— the remembrance of *Self as Spirit* and the utter surrender to meet pain with love—enlivens the *Heart's Home*. Nothing short of our *Eternal Creator Presence*, as oneness unified, heals the true cause of all suffering— perceived separation from the *direct intimate knowing* of the Heart of God.

By the time of the Dave fiasco, I had already turned more adult than my age. Yet, in secret moments, I still hoped some celestial angel or some childhood magical unicorn would shower down the rainbows that let me be a child... or a real *daughter*.

Cast aside as a scapegoat, the hope died—ending carefree, spontaneous, creative play. The toys of childhood lost meaning: enchantment felt like a lie, love felt like a lie.

Defeat.

The fantasy of childhood's adventuring frolic, morphed into trauma management.

Dave dumped his "shadow" material on my innocence and then left me to shoulder the oppressive weight of demoralization. Beyond his "personal" guilt, projected onto me, I felt the pain of the global trespass of violation of the sacred.

We can view "his shadow" as our "collective shadow" of loss of reverence. We take the shadow material, the wounding we see "out there" and see it as "in here," now embraced in the blazing *Light of Presence*.

We radically surrender the vibration, tone, or patterns of exploitation (for example). We immerse these symbolic patterns deeply in the Light of God Presence, until we feel its ultimate non-power. It becomes collectively lighter for all.

We "own" suffering or pain within, and transmute it with deep compassion. Then we "disown" it by seeing it as having no ultimate power or reality in us, or in anyone. It has no roots or wings to sustain it as we move into a new era.

I see, in *Reality*, that Dave exists as *Spirit Light*. However, his awareness of this was dimmed, denied. His perverse behavior failed to reveal his true nature.

His exploitation of the feminine child reveals a rampant and tolerated insensitivity—resulting in global violation. The life-negating virus of in-humaneness—due to perceived separation from *Light Reality*— hides under the avalanche of superficiality, pleasure-seeking and heart pain.

Scientists and prophets alike predict a potential mass extinction from the violence and war, poisoning of resources, upcoming natural disasters and such. The only answer: this world turns golden, by an en masse coming *Home to Spirit Love*, here, now in this epic pivotal moment.

Apart from doomsday or fear, what if we simply, peacefully looked at: opening the heart or perishing. *Reverence of our Creator* opens the heart, in a way that the inner kingdom of love and beauty shines.

It looms starkly obvious, that one way or another, at some point, physicality leaves us... disappears. And *all we have in that moment*, face to face with our Creator, is whatever direct luminous *Oneness with Spirit Presence* we live as.

The Eternal Love: all we have and our only trustworthy answer.

When we see how spiritual poverty spirals us downward — it fires a passion to move past *fake* love, to the *real*.

We have a huge key to spiritual realization in a very simple practice. And that involves the noticing of the small movement of "I don't want this." And the practice also involves the converse: "I do want that." The movement of this wanting or not wanting keeps the survival programs of a personal "me" alive. When this personal me stays alive, we devolve.

Forgetting that we exist as *Spirit Light* fuels the dissatisfaction, the wanting-and-not-wanting movement of the thoughts and personality. When we focus on that *movement of wanting*, it keeps us in forgetfulness of our *unmoving true nature*. That forgetfulness may range from mild selfishness, to gross transgressions.

Set your mind or affections on the things above, not of earth (Colossians 3:2) *and store up your treasures in heaven* (Matthew 6:20), perfectly aligns with *It is your Father's good pleasure to give you the kingdom* (Luke 12:32 KJV). And scripture reveals this kingdom is "within". *The kingdom of God is within you* (Luke 17:21 KJV).

Yet how do we live this?

Freedom from the habit of focus on *wanting this and not wanting that* offers a powerful key to setting the mind above, and resting as the kingdom of love and grace in the heart. This does not mean going without or *not having* in life. It means *having* through the redemption of our spiritual nature, the natural way of flourishing. *Having...* through *Being... Presence.*

When we allow the *"I don't want this" to be neutral,* and the *"I do want that" to be neutral, we feel a selfless presence that does not need to have or be anything, or act in any way upon anyone,* yet that selfless presence expresses as miracles, goodness, any giving. It is the beauty of meekness that inherits—not seeks—*inherits and shares* all things.

Humanity appears to stand at the crossroads of escalating suffering and extinction, or a radical, yet natural, awakening as *Spirit Light. The* return to *Innocence, as Spirit Light, that has and gives and that does not seek, want, or suffer—* sows the sacred seeds of the golden real life. Our total commitment to this individual and global return to *God Presence,* this *Father Ahavah Light* redemption, blesses us with safe passageway *Home in the heart.*

That passageway lies *within the heart, here, now.*

The misaligned patriarchal systems of selfishness, insensitivity, and greed have exploited the vulnerability, openness, and creative gifts of the feminine—whether that be the feminine of women, of the earth, of men, of the animals, of religion, of creativity.

The degrading force and insensitive control of the distorted masculine has suppressed the spiritual impulse.

And now there is no more "time."

Humanity is out of time.

Imagine a new expression of timeless *Divine Oneness*.

Now.

The Divine Feminine Shines
She Reveals Herself as Unstoppable in Goodness,
Victorious in Innocence
Immortal Kindness

With a Divine Breath of Gold
She Breathes a Love that Burns Away Illusions
And Soothes Away All Suffering

We Exist as One God Presence
We See This Reflection in Mary
In the Benediction of the Immaculate
Birth of Grace
Immense Love
Potent Practical Holiness
That Stops the Shattering of the Vulnerable and Innocent Ones
Commanding of Reverence

Presses Lovingly Upon all Who Walk the Earth
Creating the Crucible of Fire
That Purifies Every Masculine Essence
In Every Man, Woman and Child
Awakening All as The Sacredness, that Sees All as Sacred
And the Temple of the Feminine is Honored
And the Masculine Knows
Only the Heart of the Father Love
And the Masculine and Feminine Arise as One Life,
One Light

In Beginning
God
And God Was the Light

The Original Beginning Light
Original Light

With the Kingdom of the World of Light
Heaven's Way
Prior to This World

And the Prior To Self
Prior to Suffering
One with God Presence
Original Light

One with Eternal Father God
All Remember the Living Light
And Rest as that Holy Spirit
That Ever Loves

And Ever Gives

Alive as Father Ahavah!
Reverencing the Feminine Spirit
In all Beings

And that *Spontaneous Spirit*, the Formless Creator Light, does not *need* to form, yet may form as any beautiful physical form. Divine Life is our *real* life, before and beyond physical form.

The time will come when the "before time," "before cruelty," "before suffering," *Prior To*, way of being created, will be remembered and lived.

Imagine every woman, man, and child, every animal, plant, and mineral, and everything from the dolphins of the sea to autumn's falling leaf, from the turning toward the sunlight of the pure white lily, to the flowered garden pathways sprouting weeds, will be known as sacred.

The awareness will arise, that form reflects this spacious sacredness, this Eternal Light, this boundless beauty of Supreme Creator.

And all our pain and tears will turn to golden rain that lights the earth and turns her golden.

Envision the ineffable celestial silence, when the Immortal Ones are seen as being "still here." The soul of the saint and the light of the sage is the heart of all beings here. And we awaken as the adoration of the Eternal Father Heart of God, that smiles in everlasting goodness. The en masse global remembrance, resounds a harmonic symphony of open loving hearts.

Imagine the earth resurrect as the Christed planet she exists as, at her molten sacred core. And the sound of the Quieting tones as holiness bliss, as the only tone, the only note, the only symphony.

And even this will be seen as a pale reflection of seeing God face to face.

As the winds of unstoppable Grace, God Life Is.

This Life resurrects, deathless and free. Living Alive as Eternal Happiness, Holiness, Light, we shine.

Father Ahavah!

Experiential Application:

Light & Peace

Masculine/Feminine Kindness as One

Truth is simple.

Allow this practice to wash away former beliefs and to quicken new insights.

Yet, refrain from mentally analyzing. The human mind does not know the felt Presence of God, it does not know the answers of meeting God face to face.

We come face to face with the *Holy Light of our Creator,* as we let go of identifying as a personal "me" character.

The pain each gender feels toward the opposite gender perpetuates our global pain and spiritual amnesia. At this epic moment, a key involves healing from the abuse of the feminine and the lack of knowing the *Heart of the Father, within.*

Open to release past concepts of masculine and feminine. Embrace the highest divine reflection of these genders, while also resting in communion with God Light, in the beginning, before gender.

Every few phrases, close eyes and relax into the message.

Father Ahavah Contemplative Prayer

- Settle into a comfortable position
- Allow the breath to be slow, deep, and full
- Relax into a continuous breath, with no pause at the top of the inhale or on the bottom of the exhale
- Relax the little muscles around the eyes, and relax the muscles around the mouth
- One by one, soften and relax the face... head/scalp... jaw/neck... throat... shoulders... arms... hands... torso... back... hips... legs... feet
- Soften and relax the abdominal area...
- Imagine where you think of the spinal column to be, there is *Light & Peace... Spirit Peace...* "within" the vertebrae, and in all the muscles and nerves along the base of the skull and along the spine...
- Start at the base of the skull and slowly move awareness down the spine, contemplating *Light & Peace... Take a moment for this*
- Feel the love in your heart center and allow it to grow more and more soft and potent
- Feel the openness and tenderness in that love
- Open to the deepest remembrance of *Divine Love*, and feel that *Divine Love* as *Light & Peace*
- Open to remember original oneness with Creator, *the Heart of the Father Love, the Grace of Divine Mother Love*

- Open to the Grace of Christ's love, guiding the way of redemption from a personal "me" self
- Have awareness of this Love, as God Light, all along the spine
- This *Light* quickens the mortal body
- Imagine this *Light, Love, Peace,* along the spine and center of the body like a core column of *Light*, safety, and goodness
- And imagine this *Light* as a temple or cathedral around you - as if it expands out to the right filling the right side of the body and beyond the borders of the right side of the body... take a moment for this
- Have awareness that this *Love, Light & Peace* expands out and fills the left side of the body and expands beyond the borders of the left side of the body
- *Father Ahavah Love you exist as one with*—has no separation with you in the physical, see this *Oneness*
- Contemplate the reality of *total* security and *total* safety, as if there arises no opposite to this safeness
- Rest in being the spacious existence of *Eternal Life*... like a temple of light, the light of the world, safe
- Have awareness of the feminine principle—the strength of spiritual, mystical, creative, welcoming, grace
- Have awareness of the spiritual feminine that shatters illusions, in the same way a benevolent sword cuts away or prunes a dead branch to allow new life
- Rest as *Home*, as the *Heart of the Creator*
- Have awareness of the masculine principle—the strength of foundations, certainty generative, propelling forth

- Rest in *Adoration* of *Spirit Presence Prior To* this world, *Prior To* or before masculine *Prior To* or before feminine, yet simultaneously existing as both and expressing as either... or neither
- Rest in this... not trying to figure it out mentally...
- Feel kindness, from a feminine resonance of kindness... rest...
- Feel kindness, from a masculine resonance of kindness... rest...
- Feel kindness, from both the masculine and feminine resonance as *One*
- For example, notice the kindness may feel soft, creative, tender, spontaneous, while also firm, decisive, certain and established in strength... all interwoven at the same time
- See that masculine and feminine qualities as in harmony — rising and falling like waves in an *Ocean of Spirit Presence*, enfolding back as that, arising from that, falling back into that
- Rest in the *Ocean of Spirit Presence*, that *Light and Peace*
- *Realize that Light and Peace is before and beyond all mental-emotional-circumstantial suffering*
- Realize that in the truest reality of masculine and feminine *as one*, that neither could harm, or hurt, or exploit or dishonor the other; they honor each other as *one self*
- Have awareness of the *Feminine Spirit*... far beyond a person feeling feminine qualities, unify with the expression of the *Divine Feminine, God reflected in the feminine*
- Imagine the *Feminine* as if she only knows love and honor by the masculine

- Have awareness as masculine/feminine in perfect balance, as living light formation in perfect beauty of balance, harmony, and order
- Have awareness of existence as *Spirit Completion, before* masculine or feminine, yet able to express as *either, both, or neither*
- The masculine on earth elevates in the reflection of *Father Ahavah,*
- *Father Ahavah Presence,* ushers the way for the *Divine Feminine* on the earth, and within all, and see beings—as a beacon of Light, a platform of peace, a springboard for heaven on earth, as *God Formation*

Selah!

Chapter Nine

The Jolt:

From Jammies Shocks to The Awakening to the Time When All Was Kind

Then

Jammies are not just something that you wear.

In a sleepy unassuming way, they wear you. They characterize you. It's a jammies, jam-jams, PJs, nite-nites way of feeling, thinking... being. Of all the ten thousand things, jammies qualify as one of the best substitutes and symbols for the deepest realizations of non-doing... being *not the doer*. "I am not the doer... I am in my jammies."

Putting on jammies is like hanging out the *Do not disturb* sign on a hotel room door; it makes a statement of peace and non-disruption.

Jammies do the talking for you. They announce a culturally understood message: *"no matter what time it is, or when the moon started rising, my day is done,"* or *"no matter how long ago the sun rose, my day hasn't officially started yet."*

Pajama wearing dictates ones territory. My parents commanded: "Annie, don't *ever* go outside in your pajamas."

We owned an olive green Gremlin. It was not stylish, did not handle well, and guzzled fuel, but it provided transportation and some comic relief.

Mom habitually placed garbage bags on the Gremlin roof. She then backed the car down the driveway, got out of the car and put the trash at the curb.

One morning, still in my jammies, I curled up by the window, gently petting my copper and black cocker spaniel, Dixie. Side by side, child and dog, we looked out the window together. As we watched Mom pull out of the driveway, I giggled and whispered to my doggie, "I just know she's going to forget today."

Sure enough, the Gremlin traveled down the road with the bright white trash bag on top.

I watched to see if the trash made it back home. About an hour later, the green car rounded the bend and headed home. The top of the car: empty. I wondered, just where *did* we leave our trash today? Did it slide off on a turn and land in some unsuspecting stranger's yard? Did it spew all over a parking lot? Who had to clean it up?

In this pre-divorce time, Dad still lived in our house. I was seven, going on eight. Tensions mounted, yet the *divorce* word hadn't yet been carelessly thrown like a spear that rips at the seams of sameness and stability. Or at least the word hadn't yet fallen upon and pricked my grade school ears and little daughter feelings.

It was a combination of jammies and cheerleading jumps that set the stage for a jolting shock.

My chores and homework were long since finished when I remembered a cheerleading move I'd forgotten to practice. In the living room in my PJs, I perfected a few cartwheels and reindeer jumps, before leaping into bed for the night.

The cartwheels had a warm history. Longing to be close to my ten-year-old brother, I cheered for him when he played football in the junior league.

I tried out for cheerleading princess. I timidly stood on the field, butterflies in my stomach, hands on my hips, big breaths of anticipation, awaiting the cue to start my routine. Shy and unsure, I surveyed the football team, coaches and judges—their attentive gazes fixed upon me. My eyes fervently searched for my brother, until I discovered his exact place in the pack. He caught my eye and laughed in that way that always made me laugh in return.

Once I knew my brother was watching, I smiled with relief and started my routine. Self consciousness melted away with every jump, until I felt the rush of proud enthusiasm. Everybody loved it. As I walked away at the end, I heard things like, "She's on fire!" and "What a fox!"

I didn't know what that meant, but I felt the invisible waves of "yes!" emanating from the crowd. The beaming delight of the onlookers felt just like the sun rays smiling down on me when I played in the white capped ocean waves. Somehow, as I walked away from the tryouts, I knew I'd won, the same way you know when you *ace it* on an exam.

To feel loved and wanted flowed over me like a gentle wonderment. *Everybody loved me.* I felt sweet joy and mild fright at the same time. When alone in the quiet of my heart, I often felt this elegant feeling inside, like a beautiful swan. And yet the family "mirrors" reflected "ugly duckling" so often that my insides spiraled into little circles of confusion. I didn't feel like *badness* until they told me they saw me as unacceptable. I did not see, "Oh, this is their *projection and perception of guilt or badness, that they carry."* I learned from them that I *was* the badness. *I absorbed it.*

At the princess tryouts, a different mirror said "... not ugly, not bad," but instead, "You are a swan, innocent and graceful." Then I *felt* vindicated, and I *felt* loved, and I *felt* warmth... but I hardly dared to believe it.

The day came when, at halftime over the intercom, they announced me as the cheerleading princess. They decked me out with a royal blue velvet cape lined with white fur, a titled sash, dozens of roses and a shimmering diamond crown.

Part of me felt shy and unworthy, while another part felt peaceful. But it turned out I was a natural; I walked down the football field, graciously offering smiles and waves. Before, I was a little sister supporting my brother from the sidelines; now, I felt proud to be the *princess* cheering him on. Now, I also connected with, and loved, the crowd.

I wondered, how come I'm not celebrated at home, in my own family?

Anyway… back to the jammies, and the cartwheels.

Mom pulled up outside, with groceries in the Gremlin. During the day, I always hauled the grocery bags inside without any prompting. On this occasion, the moon had long since risen over the ebony sky, and I had pajamas on. I knew the PJ code: stay inside.

Dad suggested, "Mom's here; let's bring the groceries in." I took his comment as directed to my brother. I sweetly reminded:, "I'm in my jammies." I leapt into a cartwheel, catapulting into a traumatic father moment that shocked every part of my emotional, and physical being.

My father, shaking with rage, violently grabbed me by the leg in midair and yanked my entire body with his full bodily force.

A searing pain shot through my leg, hip and lower back. My father snarled: "get outside and get the groceries now!"

I shook and sobbed from physical pain and emotional shock.

A child is inwardly shattered over groceries.

Over an innocent comment.

Over an intention to be obedient.

Any simple comment could trigger rage, and there was no boundary—nothing to stop the rage from damaging the child, the spirit, the feminine.

This cemented an indelible imprint of trauma and pain. As a child, each aching step droned a repetitive reminder: unloved, unsafe, rejected. No one offered medical or emotional treatment for the physical and emotional injury. They persisted into adulthood.

No matter how much I "knew" that I did not deserve the abuse, on a deeper emotional level I still felt shamefully unworthy of kindness and love.

I was the badness.

And yet when I prayed, I couldn't find that badness inside.

The severe punishment generated cold shame inside, the despondence of failure. I felt crushed and violated; a sacred trust broken.

I lost the natural right to feel comfortable in my own skin—to be treated with respect. The loss of the natural right to be free of pain in my body and to receive basic nurturing, tainted my attentive love for my father.

How I wished he treasured my love! And cherished me! Without that sacred bond, I felt a deep well of sorrow, an empty sadness. The relentless scoldings and punishments demoralized me.

As the grief and resentment grew, I had to expend more effort to swallow down the sadness. I stopped practicing jumps in the house; in fact, when possible I avoided being in the living room with my dad at all. For some time, the sight of the Gremlin pulling up evoked anxiety.

I longed to run away. About two weeks after that incident, on tippy-toe I retrieved a small black satchel from the closet, and secretly packed food for my doggie and kitties. Off we went, me trying to conceal my limp, resenting the pain; my animal parade loyally trotting by my side.

We could only walk so far, but I defied the notion that I—being merely in grade school— could fail to pull this off. Still, I felt liberated and free to search for a true home out there in the world.

These risky, determined escapes all ended the same way. The olive green Gremlin pulled up, and my animals and I reluctantly climbed in. We drove back "home," hearts shutting back down, corralled, staring straight ahead.

Now

I experience compassion for my earthly Father. What reservoirs of deep pain he must have carried to inflict such misery on his own child! His unresolved bitterness rendered him incapable of living as his *True Self*. Rather than waking up in those moments to... "My God, what am I doing? I have to resolve this and find a loving way of being," he kept staring straight ahead. And thus he ignored his own pain, as well as the anguish he generated.

There is nothing "wrong" with feeling rage, feeling pain. Most beings walking on earth bear some kind of suffering. Most are feeling swirls and surges of emotions. But to believe it is okay to ignore violence—to do nothing about it—dams up the spiritual impulse to naturally love the earth and every being—to love the animals, the humans, the feminine, the masculine, the sensitive and mystical and sacred.

Now, rather than feeling that he didn't love *me*, the *me* dropped off. He didn't *know* love... in those moments, he forgot that he *is* love.

On one level, all is in perfection. When we passionately embrace spiritual reality, we live less likely to judge things as "good" or "bad". Even during the most severe trials, we often see a deepening of spiritual growth. The world may mirror our inner shadows, offering an odd kind of opportunity to dissolve shadow conditioning, darker places and fears.

On another level, the amnesia, the ignorance, the denial, the insensitivity, the trespass does not serve, and it is time to awaken. In that sense, the denial and insensitivity is not okay. We do not have to suffer in order to spiritually awaken. Nor do we need to experience pain and separation to know love. We exist as love, this instant, and are free to fully remember and be that love and that light.

It is not okay that unconsciousness and greed poison the land and the oceans, the animals, whales, dolphins, fish and birds.

It is not okay that women, and men, longing for masculine honoring, integrity, and nurturing go to bed at night with hot tears streaming down their faces, or labor under the life sentences of abuse and unhappiness.

It is not okay *to be oblivious to the pain of the abused, and drown out the feminine voice.*

It is not okay *to ignore the Divine Presence, the spiritual awakening, the only true answer.*

These cannot be okay if we wish suffering to end. We cannot live in anesthetized numbness, in denial, if we wish to live as the

Original Creation, one with God Presence, the Light of the Divine Reality.

It's time to wake up! *Awaken Now!*

We do not wake up by fighting anyone or any thing. See through this world: the separate sense of self and the needless suffering.

We set the stage for a global wake-up by forgiving ourselves for believing in this mutual, co-illusory state.

Allow the very intolerability, the clear, stark oppression of spiritual poverty, to stir a passion for spiritual awakening. When we see this fake love is intolerable, the passion for *God Union* increases. As this passion heightens, obstacles to ineffable *Eternal Love*… vanish.

And yet we need not save the world on a soap box, or get enmeshed in its dramas. As we see the world from un-anesthetized hearts, free of denial's numbness, with piercing clarity we see through the physical world of three dimensions and five senses. We behold the true, golden world, and with the eyes of Christ, we see the miraculous life.

This passion-compassion then defines us, and our life focus turns to this crystalline pure remembrance of *Self as Spirit, as Home*. And we allow the laser beams of truth and light to dissolve all that lies outside of that true Heart's Home.

Then we stand on foundations of principled truth as a tangible, lived reality. And truth puts an end to the illusions that self-interest, greed, suppression, or oppression rules us.

It's not okay that the innocent, vulnerable and sacred take the brunt of the world's abuse because the mass consciousness remains asleep to our true nature.

In one violent incident—the first episode in this book where I was struck for being too loud—my brother was not abused, although he made the most noise. The smallest and most vulnerable took the beating.

My brother and I were talking in the living room, and he was louder and even closer to my father's bedroom. He got up and left the room just as my father passed him in the hallway. It was my brother, more than me, who triggered the rage. But my dad didn't touch him.

Of course, I did not ever wish for my brother to be hit.

Yet, why did the most young, tender, vulnerable, the female, take the brunt of the abuse in the family?

Deep in the unconsciousness of humanity, the justification of crushing the very ones we most could defend and lift high... those most in need of *protection... continues...* and the core root of that — denying our sacred *God Origin as Light... continues...*

Rather than bow our hearts in divine reverence, offer our hands to the underserved and let our feet rush to protect the vulnerable... we turn our heads and cover our eyes and stare straight ahead— while speeding into the parking lot of the ice cream store.

Asleep...

While studying for my graduate degree in family therapy, I experienced a pivotal moment. Listening to a live video class on the Internet, my jaw dropped in astonishment.

The instructor discoursed on offering therapy for someone physically, emotionally, or sexually abused by his or her mother. He asserted, "That's just the worst thing, a boy molested by his mother." Then he advised, "But it's **almost okay** if *it's a girl* being abused or molested by her father or a male."

I leaped up and started to pace. Speaking aloud, I called the professor out on it. Being half Italian, I moved my whole body and hands in expressive gesture. (Fondly known as talking with ones hands).

Sheepishly I realized, *What am I doing? I am talking to a video screen!* Of a class pre-filmed earlier today!

I stopped, opening to the calm within, feeling *Presence*.

Intense frustration and grief rose from my heart, like a pulsing hot river of justice, coursing up into my throat and head. Then, dropping into the stillness, compassion emanated from my heart.

I released the anguish at the unconscious trespass of the feminine, and felt a deep passion, a longing, for the awakening of humanity, of us all. With equanimity I composed a letter to him. My heart burned with caring on this issue, while my fingers shot off intelligent sparks of unified purpose—I quickly typed my appeal.

I attended a fine university, with wise instructors. And this professor emanated good character. He stood as a Godly, admirable, caring man. Considering the source—a man I respected—rendered this oppressive statement disconcerting and even despairing.

My *for real God?!?!* letter expressed ideas like, It's not "almost okay" for the abused girl or woman who loses her*self*. It's not "almost okay" for one who feels trauma in her body in unremitting physical pain and demoralization. It's not "almost okay" for the feminine soul, aching for trust and safety, to suffer shock, distress, chronic exhaustion and loss of ability to function. It is not "almost okay" for the creative feminine to shut down, to fail to thrive, while the music of her soul *dies* in her heart. It's not "almost okay" for a woman to *lose her laugh,* her wonderment, *herself,* or the birthright experience of the divine reality. It's not "almost okay" for her to dread waking up in the morning to live another day of force, selfish oppression or domination. It's not "almost okay" for us to forget we exist as sacred in and as *God Presence.* It's not "almost okay" to perpetuate pain generation after generation —leaving a legacy of abuse and suffering—rather than a legacy of loving spiritual life and true *God Presence.*

He adamantly replied that there was *absolutely no way* he could have said that it was "almost okay" for a female to be abused; he stood unequivocally certain. As a man, as a spiritual being, as an instructor of therapists, he would *not ever* say this. In fact, he asserted that he could never even feel or think that.

However, he felt so disturbed that he vowed to go back and watch the entire videotape.

It was so unconscious that he had no clue that he believed and taught that. Yet, the *unconscious patterning tricks us like that.* The sensitive feminine *feels* when she is not being honored, even before she hears it or witnesses it. Yet, when she voices that, her appeal for heart awareness, meets walls of resistance. She is called "irrational."

Rather than *go there,* this professor had the wisdom and humility to investigate for clarity.

Initially he had no idea he even thought or felt something destructive of life.

This is how the unconscious patterning sets up little "workshops" of sabotage in all beings. It's buried so deep that life-negating and miracle-suppressing beliefs and behaviors lurk like little bandits, disclaimers of self interest, hiding in ebony shadows.

And thus there is no insight into the matrix of unconscious conditioning. The conditioning perpetuates the sense of separation from God. The unconsciousness results in the denial of injury to ourselves and each other.

And another generation dies in pain…

…Our legacy of suffering and ignorance.

Can we say: enough?

The next class, the instructor began with, "Tonight I stand corrected. Nielsen pointed something out that I did, with no idea… And I stand corrected. And all fifty of you also stand corrected because none of you even caught what I said." And then he read my letter word for word.

He proclaimed something brutal to women, and fifty other graduate students nodded their heads, staring straight ahead, not too terribly troubled. The unconscious collective thought sphere runs so deep that it has anesthetized us…

…Even the most caring and beautiful of us.

And we get shattered while anesthetized.

Trapped in a matrix of belief in the absence of Eternal Love…

Now *we* softly shatter the collective thought sphere, gently deconstruct the illusions and resurrect our remembrance. And *we rend the dense dark lie by luminously being the Reality*, by seeing the powerlessness of the illusion. We simply, peacefully exist as *the laser beam of Light*; we shine as homo luminous rising out of the ashes of homo sapiens.

When the professor took responsibility and read the letter, it restored my respect for him. Yet, it's not about "who is unconscious" and "who catches it," as if one is better than another. That is not the way.

The way is a humble adoration as *Spirit Light, and as "we" remember we support "all" as remembering.*

This is a co-forgetfulness— now a holy alchemy reaching critical mass as a co-remembrance.

The only non-fake answer calls for spiritual realization, the heart opening in authentic radical devotion. Then the identity shifts to that of *Spirit, of Light, of God Presence,* ushering in a potent laser beam of insight. This blazing clarity lays bare the unconscious while simultaneously dissolving into dust its repetitive programs. As the unconscious becomes conscious and then unwinds, *God Presence Is. The Natural Way Is.*

Spiritual leaders or loving way showers are not "better than." Yet they are not to be forgotten, or ignored, or disrespected. Offer your genuine respect to spiritual elders.

Notice how our culture lavishes submissive attentive gazes at football players and movie stars, while reaching for the TV clicker when a spiritual teacher walks on stage. No more fail to support our *Elders and Gate Keepers, who devote their lives* to usher humanity into the golden remembrance of holiness.

Honor the spiritual elders.

Perhaps they are holding the world together for us.

Singing holy canticles from humble hearts, while milking the cows at five a.m. ... so we can have our ice cream.

Where would you be without these holy ones?

Honor their immense support to end all suffering.

And stand on the brink of awakening and the threshold of *The Immensity*, and joyfully surrender to the Eternal Creator.

You cannot think your way into it. You cannot push your way into it.

You cannot run away from it.

All the ice cream will melt if it gets too hot here.

Humanity must awaken or extinguish.

And she will awaken.

Imagine and Envision
Knives That Annihilate Now Turn Into Sharing Spoons That Nurture
The Heart of Father Ahavah
Infuses All Beings & the Christed Earth
The Love of Divine Mother
Overflows Like Sweet Rivers of Peace
And Golden Spun Nectar of Honeyed Grace Dissolves All Bitterness
And Every Being

Celebrates Sacredness
And Feels Ineffable Reverence & Ecstatic Gentle Bliss
The Hearts Overflow With Giving
And The Beauty of Holiness Shines as the Eternal Original Light
Still Home
Here
Now

Father Ahavah!

And all living beings will be honored as sacred, and will light up with holy, unstoppable sentient bliss life. All will *know bliss, not as a temporary fleeting state, but as the permanent ground of being.*

And the *Freedom as Spirit* will usher in the *Golden Freedom of Home*—the freedom to love and be loved, as it was in *Original Creation... before all time... when all was kind.*

From now on, instead of hearts dying, the illusions and delusions die. The insensitivity that spurs lack of protection—of the feminine, the sacred, the open, the trusting, the trustworthy, the creative, the visionaries, the mystics—the energies that sabotage and suppress that preciousness will dissolve forever.

Now is our time, our hour, our *Holy Sacred Instant, our Now Reality* of the immortal resurrection, the deathless ascension, the unstoppable, arising of *Eternal Kindness.*

Humanity trudges on, parched and famished for the nurture of basic decent caring, for the refreshing breeze of those who take ownership and make correction, for the warmth of true integrity, for the safe flow of trustworthiness.

Let's... do... this!

Yet we "do" by undoing, by emptying, by meekness, by humility, by letting the heart break open to the *Immensity of Love, of Light* we already exist as... forever... Now.

Remember, *I Am the Light!* And let that be more Real than anything else.

Father Ahavah!

Here Now!

Selah!

Chapter Ten

How to Honor Our Dads And Be the Father Heart

Exodus 20:12, Ephesians 6:2 Honour thy father…

I am often asked: "How do I follow the scripture to 'honor' my father and mother if they abused or hurt me, or we are not close to one another?"

How can I be the *Heart of the Father?*

This honoring ushers the way for *Father Ahavah* to flood this planet, and overflow boundless blessings to you, and within you.

Let's look at ways to honor our fathers, even when we found them abusive or limited in their capacity to reveal a true *Father's Heart*. (This also applies to honoring mothers, elders, all being).

One way involves: release the past and allow a fresh, now, moment of experience. This means purifying (cleaning out) the past, and not projecting into the future. Be fully present now with positive regard. Rather than "having a relationship," simply *relate* in each moment.

Another way to honor our father involves contemplative prayer in which you inwardly greet your father as *Spirit Presence*. It merely takes an open heart and a little willingness.

Open to perceive this as his more real or more true self, as a sacred creation of God. Feel compassion (not pity) for his inability to express deeper love. And feel gratitude for the ways he did reflect this love, this more true reality of Presence.

A third way to honor our father involves letting go of a victim consciousness—see this as a global, collective, en masse spiritual anesthesia. That does not mean coddle and condone, or suppress and fester, or withhold and choke up. It means speak what needs to be shared from the heart, and open to a new experience now.

A fourth way involves the equanimity of keeping an open heart, while also honoring yourself and your true feelings about how much interaction feels right. See this inner clarity and balance, as setting a new tone on the planet. Yet, avoid the trap of the "it's all about me, my self-care is my answer" fad.

If you had a father who showed love, wisdom, commitment, kindness, and protection, then express deep heartfelt appreciation. He offered you an immense gift, to acknowledge and treasure. Actively bless him for this dedication. Consider charitable ways to support those who were not as fortunate.

If you have experienced father wounding, offer clear communication and new ways of relating, from who you are today. The key is that you offer authentic, balanced communication, rooted in your truthful experience. Welcome joining. That may range from: thank you for your wonderful fatherly influence... to, let's see if we can work through the hurts... to, let's open to a very new kind of relationship.

Center yourself in the depth of love within your heart, while also authentically and compassionately relating the impact of his attitudes and behaviors. Give yourself permission to respectfully call him to accountability, staying present in this moment. Simultaneously, with humility, open to self insight and take ownership of your own inner healing and transformation. The world needs more beings who take ownership, who offer accountability for how they impact others.

He may not "father" "you" in a more deep or fulfilling way at this time. He will respond from his present state, his current ability to show love. If he offers a hollow feeling connection, then simply release the attempt at this time, and discover even more deeply the endless wellspring of *Father Ahavah*, within. Share this inner love in the same way the sun shines its warming light upon all.

You exist as *ultimately fulfilled in oneness with Holy Spirit Life, one with Father Spirit.* This stands true regardless of the attitudes and behaviors of your father or anyone. Deepen in total reverence. *Feel reverenced* by the Divine Presence, and abide in this "within."

No human father can give you what *Father Ahavah*, Creator God Father gives you and *is* to you. And that gift is already given to you — in being created in the very image and exact likeness of the Eternal Love, Light.

There is something about the *Divine Feminine (Mary, Father God of Compassion, Divine Mother)* coursing through the woman, and that being honored and reverenced — every fresh miracle illumines every sentient being and all the earth. And there is something critically significant in this hour about the *Divine Feminine* infusing every essence of a woman—and that being neglected, dishonored, and disgraced. This pulses as a universal travail, inexorably invoking redemptive grace on the earth.

We are in the delivery room at the moment of birth.

We feel the bearing down of birth pangs, the global contractions pushing closer together, enlivening this christened nativity: *honor the feminine*. We feel the renewed covenant of this global quest: return to the *Heart of the Father*.

This primordial longing, morphs into a sword of fire that resurrects the divine feminine and her masculine with her, truly, truly… this time… *with her*.

At times it felt destabilizing to feel profoundly cherished in *God Presence*—and *simultaneously* heartbroken by being objectified with gross insensitivity. I witnessed so many of us focused on survival, competition, jealously, and mistrust. Yet in deeper potency of ineffable *Holy Presence*, the joy of overflowing giving, sparked the serene satisfaction of *completion*.

Part of honoring our fathers stems from uprooting resentment from the failure to thrive under his lack of nurture. Open to compassion for any unconscious resistance or fear he felt in providing for his progeny. When a man (or being) forgets their true nature of love and giving, then loyalty, and support, contracts into fear and withholding. The father who feels separate or disconnected from God Presence experiences contraction and suffering. He consciously or unconsciously justifies his withholding.

Withholding is not a spiritual principle. Pause to allow any pain from feeling withheld from, to arise, be met with love and released. No matter what we name as the object withheld (from respect to a new pair of jeans, from affection to more financial prosperity, from adoration to acknowledgment) beneath this lies a belief in the *absence* of love. Because that thing remained withheld, we felt unloved, or fearful. Yet our belief in the absence of love, unwittingly, perpetuates more of these same life disappointments.

Forgive, release judgment or grief from whatever you *longed for* and felt an *absence of*. Rest in a deeper freedom in knowing the spiritual reality—being, having, giving—as, and in love.

At all levels of your being shift *source* and *resource* from father or mother, from spouse or child, from this world to the oneness with Creator Presence, as present and unlimited resource.

Christ urged beings to "take no thought for your life" (Matt 6:25 KJV) for "it is the Father's great happiness to give you the kingdom" (Luke 12:32 NLT).

His messianic message revealed "the kingdom of God *is within you*" (Luke 17:21 KJV, italics added).

The psalmist proclaims "my cup runs over… surely goodness and mercy follows me all the days of my life" (Psalm 23). Let the bitter empty cup of withholding fade into the bright radiant love of *Father Ahavah's* way—endless blessings from the kingdom of Spirit within. Behold merciful outcomes in life.

Then the release from our wounds from withholding, anoints us for the epic honoring—*Father Ahavah* honoring.

Honor your father by contemplating release and healing of all ancestral and family conditioning. Hold a prayerful vision of all ancestors, in reverence of our Creator. See in your prayer the reality of God Presence as *more real* than anything or anyone of any time, or any generation.

Have compassion—the belief in withholding binds the father in a forgetfulness of his prosperous spiritual nature. Yet, *Eternal Father* reveals abundant having and spontaneous sharing.

Open now to directly be that warm, golden *Father Spirit Light*, and to see all men (and women) as this Light in reality. Feel the heart smile at this silent, sacred gift you offer. What beautiful eyes you have, looking out upon the reality of love and giving, that our fathers and all beings truly exist as at their core.

This knowing simultaneously sends a message to the heart of the daughters and sons of life that they exist as this infinite giving, free of withholding. *True Spirit Self* exists as God Presence, as causeless happiness and effortless flourishing.

Releasing Dishonor

No matter how severe the trauma imprints— you now have the capacity to serve and make a difference for others. In fact, *because* you know the anguish of the shattering of what you most loved or needed; and *because* you responded to that by radical surrender into the *Heart of the Eternal Father*, then you speak with a power that summons radical shifts in all hearts. Our *response* deems our life successful, not what happens to us. Go deep in emptying all wounds, to live as the clear transparence— luminous clarity and genius.

It takes perseverance, and it is well worth it.

Though the "suffering" lessened—from less belief in the story or commentary— the sensations of pain, from enduring disrespect, did not magically stop.

Initially, being dishonored evoked pain. However, as I persisted, being dishonored *stopped, stopping me.*

It *stopped stopping me* from radically surrendering a personal "me" to die into God. It *stopped stopping me* from seeing all beings as Light, no matter how incapable of love and honor they acted. And it *stopped stopping me* from being an immensity of sacred loving service, offering wisdom, grace and compassion.

And after that, it stopped being painful… not before.

And after it stopped stopping me and it stopped being painful, for the most part it stopped showing up. And when it did show up, it afterward led to some kind of life promotion or surprise gold nugget of good fortune.

It *stopped stopping me* from being the "I Am" beyond a "me". It stopped stopping "I" from being Light, from being Love, from being the light of the world.

Honor Father By Seeing The Reality of Spirit Light

Through the years, I sat for hundreds of hours, seeing through who my earth father was as a man and… really deeply seeing him… as *Spirit Light*.

I knew that as the highest sacred service, the most loving grace.

It sparked rich remembrance of what he and I both truly exist as, beneath whatever stories, or shadows, happened.

And one day I felt a deep release of him on every level. And the identity as daughter - as rejected and withheld from—faded, and the identity born as *Eternal Father,* as eternal daughter shimmered in joy.

We do not have to necessarily have contact with someone physically to honor them. However, when we fully release we are free to respond with care and love if they reach out to us.

Releasing judgment does not mean ignoring wisdom or discarding discernment, or crossing intelligent boundaries. It means releasing a harsh or negative point of observation of another. We drop the face value, appearance based, cynical, unkind view.

Forgiveness, releasing judgment, means perceiving the abuse as more than one odd dad in denial, it involves an entire species under deception… *largely… lost inside.*

If humans feel separate from inner spirit essence, and disconnected from Eternal Creator, then they *will hurt* each other. If we identify as a personality in a body that dies, separate from Eternal Life Presence, then there *will be fear*. And when fear rules, love disappears. When love disappears, trespass happens.

Yet, love does not ever disappear, and we do not die.

Homo sapiens thinks so. And thus, it seems so.

Until the quickening life of Spirit resurrects us as homo luminous… and then… *Homo Light.*

The genus of Light.

Original Light.

Origin: Light.

Who are you? What birthed you?

Homo sapiens in suffering birthed you? Or Eternal Creator, Origin of Light?

Who is dad? What birthed him?

Homo grandparents? Or Eternal Creator, Origin of Light?

This is true forgiveness. True honoring.

<u>Fake forgiveness, hollow honoring looks like this</u>: "I am a personality in this body, and this other gender person or parent hurt me... because... well... they are disconnected and don't know how to love. And I, being more loving and better, will forgive them...yet I know how inferior they are and they are lucky that I won't hold things against them... even though I would never do what they do.

<u>Prodigious forgiveness, epic honoring looks like this:</u> "Emotional pain is released with clear perception of emotions as programs, aimed at survival. I acknowledge suffering's persistent questioning undertow and answer with radical love for *God Presence. Radical love... deep knowing reverence.* With clarity, I see the aching longing to be handled as sacred, to be loved. I now see suffering's cause as a misidentification of spiritual nature. Yet, Eternal Love, *Divine Original Father, Is.* As a personal "me" fades, and there arises this ineffable holy Presence, Oneness with God, my whole being feels the wonder and joy of this Spirit Light. Open and surrendered, this *Divine Original Father* illumines my

heart... and I feel immaculately and safely *Home*... as *Eternal Love*. God Light exists as the reality of my father. The focus stays not on dad, not on personal "me", not on the ten thousand things of the world... passionate laser beam focus remains on/in the *Eternal One*.

There exists no strong identification as a personality, a woman, (a being) who had or didn't have a dad. The direct experience pervades as God's daughter (son), heaven's offspring, the daughter of the fire of Spirit, the daughter of the *Holy One of Light*.

It is the scriptural injunction of "I no longer live...Christ lives in me." I (personal me) no longer runs the show, God Presence, Light, lives me. The "me" identity based on thoughts, perceptions, memories, imprints, fades. And the "I" as *"I Am That"* Oneness with *God Presence* identity arises.

That peace prevails of being one with the *I Am*. And the peace prevails of seeing father, seeing men, seeing all, as the *I Am, Spirit Life*.

We honor our fathers, ourselves and all on earth by awakening within to the *Heart of the Father, in this context of this world*.

It's the awareness: *I exist as so one with Father Ahavah, I identify with and as that*.

We honor our fathers, ourselves and all on earth by being the heart of the daughter. This means authentic communication, soft release of judgment, remembering according to our earth dad's best "sides" which is their Spirit "Sides."

We honor our earth dads by having compassion for the disappointments in life, the struggles or pressures, or his inability to receive *Grace*.

We all feel pain. We all long for *Grace*.

Honoring our earth dad epic style means sitting in stillness, with awareness of him as *Spirit Light*. And do this regardless of whether you felt honored by him or rejected.

See that perhaps he loved his daughter in some way better than his Dad loved him.

To honor our dads see the story, embrace it and then release it to move beyond stories. The vignettes in this book are not intended as personal stories of personal people. They offer a screenshot of the global condition, for us un-anesthetize, in the living fire of the sacred heart.

There comes a time to see that for the human mind, any story will do and all the stories are the same. The mind perpetually creates a story of the character, a separate sense of a "me" that things happen to. And none of it has truth in ultimate reality, in the kingdom within, the eternal reality. In a grander, wider, view, *Spirit Is*, in all beauty and joy, all peace and perfection. Yet we have to profoundly know that to break free of the matrix of our dream of duality.

The highest honoring of our fathers, our elders and our planet lies in investing our roulette chips of focus, attention and devotion in the eternal treasures. Christ called this storing up treasures "above." Once you see that apart from *Spirit Life*, the decks are stacked, the House—the Casino (this world)—always wins, in the end. If we live disconnected from *Eternal Presence*, life here unfolds as moments of pleasure, and long periods of pain. And then we come to the *final moment* of the 6x3 foot box beneath the earth. No matter how ornate our casket, and how flowery the tombstone inscription... *then what*?

We know this. Look at all the bodies in the world, where will they all be in 100 years? We know this... yet do we *intelligently look* at this?

What lasts?

What is our legacy?

Honor our fathers, our ancestors, and all beings by leaving a legacy of Light, of spiritual remembrance. Leave the eternal legacy of *Being Father Ahavah Presence*.

And more significant than leaving a legacy, is leaving this world, at some future time, *as The Legacy... Eternal*.

Once you stand convinced of the vanity of this world apart from that *Spirit Life*—the temporariness of this world, the superficiality of it, then you are "doomed-blessed" and "anointed-christened" as one of the *deep ones*.

Forget the hollow.

Join our family of the deep ones.

Come Home in the Heart.

You see there is no where to go other than the true *Home*; and this world as perceived through the lenses of lack and separation, is not true *Home*. Yet, abiding as *Home*, this world exquisitely shines in the luminosity, and the grace of *Home*.

We are camping out here. Yet while we are camping here, passing through here, we may reflect the Glory of God. We awaken as the exquisite Holiness of The Divine, we spark the ending of pain throughout this world and all universes and galaxies.

We were "birthed," in this world, yet not born here. One with *Father Ahavah*, we come alive as Eternity… Unborn Light. We merge in this ineffable *Father Heart, as the Father Heart, with the Mother Heart, as the Mother Heart, yet existing as that Light before Mother Father.*

"*In the beginning was the Light… and that Light was the Light of all men.*"

"*God is Light, and in Him is no darkness*" (no lack of Light).

In reality all we ever really have is the *Home of Light in* our *Hearts… that light house that guides us to the ever pulsing heart beat of Eternal Love.*

All we ever really have is the changeless *Eternal Reality, the Original Innocence, the Living Light.*

And we are still *Home*.

Somehow we dream, we imagine we are in exile.

We are *Home,* dreaming of exile.

And when we awaken we will see:

I am awake now! My dream has not occurred. *I Am Still Home….*

Home in the Heart…

Father Ahavah!

Selah!

Chapter Eleven

The Return of the Heart of the Father

The emergence of the redeemed feminine spirit calls the masculine home to love. And the return of the father's heart, the masculine heart, elevates and nurtures the feminine home to love.

We each have the capacity to express characteristics of our opposite gender. Our male- female gender-sparked relationship challenges—wherein women feel hurt by men and men by women—heal in two key ways. One way involves our spiritual realization as *Presence* beyond genders. Another invites us to balance the masculine and feminine characteristics within ourselves. From this equanimity and completion, we usher in the highest synergy and flow with those of opposite gender.

We exist as *Spirit Presence*—before and beyond all gender.

In beginning… *Light Is*.

And that *Light* existed before masculine or feminine gender. We may call this the *Prior To* Light *or Prior To* Presence. It is the Light of the *Heart of the Father* before there were fathers.

God Is, Light Is.

Light formed into the sun, which is and gives light, thus, there is a light *Prior To* sun.

In a similar way, the *Light of the Father Is. Father Ahavah, Original Father Light Is, as* formless light.

Prior To.

Rather than grasping this mentally, open to *feel it as a knowing*.

It is the *Father Light* just *Prior To* what we see as the Father Heart of God, the Mother Heart of God. This arises similar to *the Light*, before the Light of the sun and the moon - that is before sun or moon, yet can form as sun or moon. This does not compare God Presence to the sun or moon, it offers an analogy about one thing prior to another—Light prior to Light form... prior to form.

The *Father Ahavah!* The Eternal Light!

This Original Light *knows*. It is the *Living Light*, the *Name above all Names, Nameless One*.

It is not far off, distant, unavailable or unresponsive. The *Heart of the Father* is here now, closer than our breath, more real than our minds or bodies or world. It lives us, breathes us, with intimate, cherishing, potent love—present, available. This constitutes epic responsiveness—Oneness.

The *Heart of the Father* knows. It knows every salty tear of longing and turns it into rainbows of Living Light.

The *Heart of the Father* knows. It knows every need before it arises and answers the need.

The *Heart of the Father* knows. It knows how to love, nurture, and bless every living son and daughter to flourish in integrity, joy and peace.

The *Heart of the Father* knows. It guides with wisdom. It leads by holding the *Presence* in such stillness that everything rises up to that ineffable quiet.

The *Heart of the Father* knows. It can be trusted.

The *Heart of the Father* knows. It knows exactly how to call forth the simplicity, goodness, and magnificence of the hearts of its offspring, its creations, its daughters and its sons.

The *Heart of the Father* knows. It uplifts without chains. It nurtures without weakening. It exalts without arrogance, it protects without spoiling.

The *Heart of the Father* knows. It sees perfection and sees innocence. It is the tone of honor and reverence.

The Heart of the Father knows.

The *Heart of the Father knows* how to behold its daughters and its sons as an immensity of sacred, breathtakingly stunning Light. And when the daughters and sons of *God Presence* awaken to and respond to this holy gaze... *they remember.*

I AM That!

Father Ahavah!

To be known by the Heart of the Father is to awaken, to be, the Father Heart, and call all to this Father Heart.

Everything starts with coming *Home*. That is not the end destination; it is where we begin. And yet, it's where we already are... *still*.

Still Home!

Begin each day, each hour, each moment, aware of the peaceful freedom of dissolving the perceived separation from the Heart of Father God. Feel *Papa Spirit* as close as the breath. Deeply embrace that *Presence*, here now.

Feel it as you, *the Now Reality*, upon which all thoughts, feelings, events, and relationships seem to arise... to rise, fall, ebb, flow.

Know Father Heart, at the core, as the Heart of Existence.

Whatever Name we give this Supreme Presence, we now remember this intimate *knowing of It*. It is Papa, Adonai, Holy Spirit, Great Spirit, I Am that I Am (Holy Name of God—Ehyeh Asher Ehyeh), Divine Mother, Holy One.

To know *Self* as one with *That*, in ineffable adoration and reverence, is our authentic answer.

As you know the *Heart of the Father*, profound awakening dawns. Each holy instant arises christened as true Home. You then behold Self as the safe haven for so many daughters and so many sons hurting so badly. And then the daughters and sons quickly come Home.

And then you are being the Heart of the Father for all the fathers who longed to have that father heart and could not find their way there.

Live and be the return of the Heart of the Father.

Father Ahavah!

Selah!

Chapter Twelve

Fathers Provoke Not Your Children to Wrath: Daughters And Sons Live As Father Spirit of Courageous Innocence

One of the greatest losses for the daughter or son enduring a disapproving, critical father, or other unkind masculine influences— is the *provoking to wrath*.

Scripture verses encourage fathers to not provoke or embitter their daughters, or children. "Fathers, provoke not your children to wrath, but bring them up in the nurture and admonition of the Lord" (Ephesians 6:4 KJV). "Fathers, do not provoke your children, lest they become discouraged" (Colossians 3:21.). One translation conveys: "do not *embitter*…".

"Fathers, do not irritate and provoke your children to anger (do not exasperate them to resentment) but rear them (tenderly) in the training and discipline and the counsel and admonition of the Lord"(Ephesians 6:4, Amplified Version).

We thus have a distinction between ways that lack fatherliness — that *provoke to wrath, embitter, and that exasperate to resentment* — such as judgment, criticism, abuse, stubbornness, not hearing. And we have tender ways of fatherliness (or motherliness) or general caring, that foster growth in grace and assurance.

Rather than provoke to wrath, protect with nurturing.

If fathers are, if we collectively are, *Being One With God Presence*, then we inspire those around us with a passion to *Be Presence*.

Presence invokes Presence...rather than wrath provokes wrath... conflict and suffering... ad infinitum.

Invoke Presence. Rather than provoke pain.

"Fathers provoke not your children" seems counterintuitive to another verse, often misinterpreted, to condone disciplining children by hitting them. The notorious verse used to justify spanking: "spare the rod, spoil the child," (based on Proverbs 13:24) does not unequivocally exhort parents to beat a child with a stick. We cannot casually assume this means to spank, hit, or beat a child. Other interpretations exist. The rod, staff, or scepter provides teaching, guidance, protection and loving authority.

"Yea, though I walk through the valley of the shadow of death, I will fear no evil; for thou art with me; thy rod and thy staff they *comfort* me" (Psalm 23:4, italics added).

Use the staff of truth to comfort, to dispel destructive patterns— not to destroy sentient persons. The scepter, or staff of spiritual principle, can dispel deceptions, or ignorance, by the laser beam of truth, the revealing power of Light that undoes the shadow sides.

The "rod" described a handsomely and meticulously carved wooden staff. The highly esteemed staff revealed the treasures of beautifully crafted Torah scriptures, loving spiritual principles, engraved in the wood. A parent sat by the child's side, holding this sacred staff, and recited the carved ancient scriptures. And the parental guide lovingly instructed the child in spiritual life, devotion and wisdom. Guidance unfolded as: observe before you the ways of spiritual *life*, and see clearly the ways set before you of destruction (death). Choose the natural way of principle, of *Presence*. Nurtured with wisdom, the child aspired to the ways of goodness, mercy, and reverence.

We *ache* for this fatherly holy wisdom… this smiling tenderness… this watchful gaze of attentiveness… this passionately protective guidance.

We long for this like the ocean longs for its salt and the flower longs for its fragrance and the human longs for its breath. It stands as *that* integral to our beingness. It is right here within our hearts, and the center-point to the divine order of our innermost core.

We long to be seen as holy and observed as sacred.

And then we infinitely and prolifically flourish in the nourishment of this *Divine Father Love*.

We as individuals, as families, as communities, as countries, suffer in our *global lack of sacredness… our global lack of direct experience of Divine Father Love*.

We could not move further away from sacredness than denying abuse, and perpetuating violence.

Sacredness unifies.

Violence shatters.

Even more covert forms of violence — rejecting indifference, emotional cruelty, punishing blame—provoke to wrath, and/or beats into submission. It crushes the bud of the heart, choking its eternal peace and the power of its brilliant contribution. Thus, provoking to wrath—to unhappy duress—occurs in overt abuse as well as more subtle forms of dismissive neglect.

A girl or woman (or the feminine side within men) innately feels enchanted inspiration. The feminine expresses as open, vulnerable trust, and creative giving.

The exquisite peace of God Union—the tangible trust in the Divine Presence —is the natural way. However, in our collective unconsciousness of ignorance, a "personal me" fear-based parent trains a "personal me" child—to want, seek, lack, try, earn—while getting disapproved of, criticized and/or simply inwardly disconnected from spiritual life. This constitutes our unnatural way that proves unsustainable.

And in this provoking to wrath and lack... *our inward and outward pool of unsolved global agonies continues.*

When the feminine one is rejected, abused, mistreated, this fires up frustration and resentment. The unremitting invalidation escalates, and the resentment turns to animosity, and to despair.

The greatest tragedy of violence and abuse is that its dense, distasteful suffocating signature and smell, sears in a belief in actual separation from God.

And the soft, tender, creative one contracts… and contracts… and the heart chokes… and hardens… and dies.

Rejection brings rebellion.

We attribute this rejection unto God. On some level, a person projects God as distant or God as punitive, or God as unresponsive.

Abuse perpetuates the sense of *separation from divinity* as the core essence. It seems to prove we are not holy, not one with God, not sacred, not the Light. It makes a set-in-stone case for guilt, rather than allowing the natural *Oneness with Immaculate God Innocence* to shine.

Rather than the acceptance of sacredness, abuse engenders the shame of rejecting the self as unholy. Abuse imprints its message: you are not precious, you are not a treasure… *you are nothing and do not mean much.*

One of the most painful duresses that the innocence, and creative giving of the feminine experiences, is the masculine seeing her as much less than she is. Her kindness is viewed as *weakness*. Her creativity is depicted as *irrational*. Her trustingness is *exploited*. Her aspirations meet with a wall of resistance. Her visions invoke inflammatory questioning and censure.

This is *the pain, the global pain,* of our collective condition. We hurt inside, longing for this *Father Ahavah Love* that joins us in communion, and deep compassion.

No battle or competition exists in this *Father God Presence* love.

Love that has to be battled for isn't really love.

Stop once and for all ever battling for or seeking love. Or approval or security or safety. No actual absence from profound love exists. Not ever. Not for one instant. Not now… not in the future… not in the past… not ever.

Each moment we experience that non-absence of love, we develop immunity to being provoked to wrath. As stored emotions release, as beliefs purify, and as *Being Divine Love arises as the True Self*… wrath dissolves into oceans of compassion and honor.

Love Is.

Abiding as that *Eternal Love,* all need evaporates to seek, chase or attain love. Courage arises to call self and those around you to accountability and ownership of unconscious patterns. Humans mistreated by the masculine may smolder in hard-to-erase animosity, swirl in reservoirs of sadness, deflate in pushed-beyond-limits tiredness.

Beneath this anger lies a deep grief, sorrow and sense of loss. Often this loss stems from feeling a loss of the heart rest, the sweetness, the natural expression of reverence, wonder, and glory.

Deep connection to the *Heart of Father God, Father Light, Original Papa Spirit of all Eternal Love* washes away the anger and bathes the heart in heaven's nectar.

A flourishing life then arises, fresh and new each instant.

Fathers, men, provoke not your children, your daughters, your wives, your ladies to wrath. Let them feel protected, cherished, honored, esteemed.

Fathers, men, women, provoke not the masculine sons to wrath. Honor, respect, and welcome them to the highest principles of grand life.

And daughters, feel the softness happening on the "inside" when you feel the safe sanctuary of: no one can "give" or "take away". Allow that feminine grace and beauty to luminously ignite happiness. Invoke relationships to honor that, and mirror that.

And sons, open to the masculine signature of *Father Ahavah's* love, and be the light of the world— courageous in righteousness, amidst a world of darkness, shadows and pain.

Break free. Feel any suppressed percolating anger from betrayal. Open the heart again and again; refuse to close the heart around the hurt. Surrender to the heartbreak beneath the wrath, and feel it to its full depth. Open the space, and be with it, and live as the *Courageous Innocence Presence*, safe and free.

Both masculine and feminine embody the inner spirit essence of *the truth salve. This* forever washes away the ancestral and global wall of denial that provokes to wrath.

That salve, that elixir of grace, consists of the *essence of innocence and the essence of courageousness*. This shifts the provoking to wrath to the awakening as *Father Ahavah*.

Experiential Application:

The Courageous Innocence

Father Ahavah Contemplative Prayer

- Relax in a comfortable rested position
- Allow the breath to be full, deep, slow, with at least several seconds on the inhale and several seconds on the exhale (through the nose)
- Soften the face... relax the shoulders
- Allow the body to be as limp as a rag doll, yet, present and attentive
- Have an awareness of oneness with *Eternal Love*
- *Simply softy contemplate... Spirit Is... Light Is... Eternal Love Is...* "falling back" into *That*
- Remember oneness with *That Holy Presence... deeper than ever before*
- Have awareness of our Creator as *Changeless Innocence...* remember oneness with *The Creator* and *Innocence*
- Feel the powerful and tender reverence within *The Innocence...*
- Have awareness of the place in you that *knows* the essence of *Holy Innocence... is this Innocence*

- Have awareness of the place in you that *knows* the essence of *Divine Courageousness… is Spirit, which is the Presence of Courageousness*
- Rest as Innocence… allow it to blossom more and more… rest in this for a moment
- Feel Courageousness… allow the experience of Courageousness to grow potent… rest in this for a moment
- Feel *Innocence and Courageousness* as one blended essence… a rarefied divine feeling… changeless natural way… *Presence*
- Have awareness of existence as Spirit that is *Innocence Essence, Courageousness Essence*… beyond all thoughts, emotions, or situations
- Feel the changeless, eternal Spirit of *Innocence Courageousness*
- Imagine the image of your father (or any male figure with which you have unresolved emotion)
- If you prefer, this image can be an inch tall, fifty feet away and have its back to you, or imagine the image closer, larger, facing you
- Find the comfortable way to imagine the image
- As this *Courageousness Innocence Presence* have awareness of any emotions that arise
- Rather than looking out as the personality "me" seeeing the image, looking out as *Presence as Courageousness Innocence*
- See the image of father or male figure, and notice anything that throws you off balance, or creates a resistance or contraction

- Sit very still inside, welcoming these feelings, resistances, and contractions
- Allow what wishes to be seen and met, the buried feelings or fears, to rise... to be met with love... soften, flow and dissolve
- Notice any provoking to anger and the residues of resentment or reservoirs of bitterness... release... rest...
- Allow these thoughts, emotions, to dissolve into an ocean of *Courageousness Innocence*
- Take a few moments for this
- *Presence* envelops, embraces, and heals-enlivens all of you
- Scan your body and notice any contractions, any unpleasantness in the body as you see the image of your dad or male figure
- Release these contractions, relax into a safe peaceful feeling within
- Allow this safe, love, peace feeling within to grow stronger, even in the "presence" of the image of a masculine figure around which you suffered
- Now forget the image for a moment and open to feel this *Courageousness Innocence*...rest as that for a moment or two
- As you again think of the image of your father (or this person) feel *Self as Courageousness Innocence*, until the feeling is as potent and strong as when you are not imagining the image of person... with no wobble, no loss of certainty or peace
- Realize, "this person or relationship does not define me"
- *I Exist as One With Father Ahavah*... that does not provoke to wrath... *Eternal Love... the true ground of being*

- Open to the embrace of this indivisible, undiminished sameness of Love
- If you wish, have an awareness that no matter how much fear or mistreatment dad or this person may have shown, at the core essence they are *Courageousness Innocence*, that *is* love and that at some higher spiritual reality, knows the *Innocence, the Light of you*
- See that the *Light to Light, the Innocence Courageousness* knowing *Innocence Courageousness is* more real than anything else, and rest in that without having to change or reconcile anything of the physical, material situation
- Simply know this on the inside, without having to take any actions
- Release all images of all persons and the attention to personality-body "me" and feel the "I" as Spirit
- This "I" Self is Spirit, Holiness, Changeless Joy
- Rest as this *Spirit aware of Spirit*
- Rest as this *Innocence Courageousness Aware of Innocence Courageousness* as if there is nothing else… abide as that
- Father Ahavah!

Selah!

Chapter Thirteen

"I Want a Daddy So Badly"

I saw in myself, and in so many others—often independent, giving, and accomplished persons—a suppressed, buried longing of "wanting a daddy so badly."

Executive women parading in two-thousand-dollar suits, magazine models lounging in bikinis, famous women signing autographs, obscure women isolating from life, simple women enjoying tea in their small garden, atheist women disenchanted with God, spiritual women awakening as Light—all express astonishment at the fountainhead gush of this forgotten forlorn force called "wanting a daddy." It lies like a sleeping dragon of bewitching languor, feigning contentment when anesthetized, yet now and then rumbling awake with a quest for freedom. Yet, as it awakens, opens, and unleashes into the redemptive embrace of *Father Ahavah*, it is the most sweet, innocent, natural rise to fulfillment.

This hidden want also swirls deeply in many men. These sons crave a more affirming father bond, a strong imprinting of the masculine, a deeper honoring of their mother by their fathers, an authentic affirmation of their masculine expression. I have witnessed men crushed by their father telling them they would not amount to anything in life.

A daddy.

Even those who had present, loving fathers, on some level long for spiritual fathering. Our culture has largely lost our father-sage-eldership that spiritual communities and tribes championed.

Spiritual fathership.

For a small daughter or son, if the warm, wise and protective Papa presence is not there—whether through a father dying, or leaving, or being harsh/critical/abusive—this imprints in the psyche, the thought sphere, the emotional body, the physical cellular level.

This father hunger hollows out an unhappy ache in the heart.

It takes on a life of its own.

Our deepest unhealed wounds solidify into convictions. These self-beliefs project outward in the same way a megaphone carries sound waves across distance. These energy webs spiral out invisible, yet detectable, frequencies (like radio frequencies in the air waves) that extend beyond the borders of our physical bodies. We culturally refer to it as the "vibe." The thoughts, emotions, beliefs, and sensations weave an energetic field a few feet around us.

For the unfathered ones this may radiate a field of sorrows from loss of protection. It leaves a signature of lost, forgotten, frustrated, alone, unprotected. The whole field of being yearns for sweet, powerful father nurturing and the passing down of rich family heritage.

This devoid-of-father energetic field dilutes us. Yet, it simultaneously smothers us like a suffocating cocoon of doubt, or a support-repelling electrical fence of hardship. It deters respect and compassionate support, and perpetuates obstacles.

When a father withholds affirming nurture from his progeny, the child's memories and feelings of pain then weaken the inner respect and outer boundaries. This creates a vulnerability in life and an unconscious repetition of unsupportive relationships.

It sends out the signals of the "absent" nurturing masculine. And it may translate as a core emotion, or as a triad of belief-emotion-mentation. For example, the unresolved emotions of loss-sadness-resentment, may generate thoughts of "I never get what I want", bonded to "it's no use", woven with "no use trying".

Scientific research now reveals that the exact resonance of our emotions in our cells, shows up in our DNA—even if that DNA is put into a beaker and transported miles away. Refined instruments detect our field of measurable energy wave patterns. Our energetic field holds imprints from the cells, psyche, mind, emotions. All of these may factor into our sowing and reaping, envisioning and creating, which we see play out in our life story—our "real life" movies.

The matrix of suffering and want, flashes invisible neon signs that message the universe: *father hunger*. It may send the signals of one primary symbolic emotion—such as a field of sadness, a field of frustration, or a field of loneliness. Or it may emanate as a tribe of beliefs, thoughts, and emotions bonded as a triad—such as disappointment-resentment-regret or animosity-sorrow-anguish, or loss-depression-withdrawal, or doubt-timidity-despair.

And yet... all the while... we exist as *still* one with *Father Ahavah!*

Creator, Spirit Light, of joy, freedom, and grace—shines as our redemptive power of limitless goodness. This *Eternal Presence* creates an immortal field of living light, within and around our whole being. We then express as glory, and we reveal the beauty of a potent reverence.

Protection now.

And that occurs as the mental-emotional conditioned "me" is identified with (owned) ; then dis-identified with (disowned) as not the primary identity. Yet, the owning and disowning have soft lines, as if the *Father Ahavah* warm embrace, merges the personal conditioned suffering "me" into *Itself.*

Home now.

In the potent *Light of Spirit Presence,* the imprints soften, fade and dissolve from within the mental-emotional, cellular, and energetic field. They are not based on ultimate reality and they have no true power. As the *wounded daughter or wounded son* identity merges with the identity of *Father Spirit,* the entire energetic field blazes with *Golden Presence.*

You are the Light of the world.

Experiential Application:

Dissolve "I Want a Daddy so Badly"

Abide as Story Free Self-Completion

Very often the "wanting a daddy, or longing for spiritual fathering feeling" is masked by apathy, rigid independence, or gaining significance by care-taking others.

We may have unconscious programming: *fixing others, fixing men, fixing men's messes or problems, rescuing a partner of any gender, or over-giving to any gender.* These hidden patterns form in the psyche as survival programs aimed at avoiding abandonment. We may end up in relationships that fail to honor us, or match our sincere commitment.

Notice inner pressure to care-take or to be over-responsible for others. Inquire if giving is from joyful inspiration, or a subtle attempt to feel needed, significant, and valued. We try too hard to be loved, strive to prove our worth, when all the while we have infinite inherent worth. When we historically cannot depend upon others to follow through or care, we may feel we have to manage and control situations.

No need to try too hard to be loved…

No need to try at all to be loved… ever…

Be Love.

And Rest in That.

Rather than attempting to be loved and unwittingly moving into a control or approval seeking mode, deepen in *being Love happening on the inside. Be Love Presence.* And be the mindful gatekeeper to watch and observe, who coming into your space, are the best ones to open the heart to? Who can reciprocate honoring love and respect?

If the *I want a Daddy so badly* still operates— allow those thoughts-feelings-sufferings to have the space to arise and fade. With compassion, really detect it, observe it, and release it.

In *Spirit Reality*, no lack exists, nothing is missing or withheld. Remember: *Spirit Presence, total eternal completion, here now...* is the real.

Father Ahavah Contemplation

- Simply relax, breathe deeply and slowly
- Have little interest in thoughts... allow the mind to quiet
- See thoughts or emotions as arisings, which fade into background
- Place awareness on the breath for a moment... simply place all attention only upon the slow deep inhale and exhale
- Even focusing for two minutes on the breath may quiet the mind chatter by eighty percent
- As the mind stills and quiets, *Sprit Presence* feels more real to us than thoughts or emotions

- Be the awareness, aware of feelings, yet without diving into the feeling...
- Rather than identifying as the energetic content, *be the one aware* of the energetic content
- This allows space between you as Presence and the emotion or content
- Realize: I am not the content of experience; I am the one aware of it
- And simply have awareness of emotions—sadness? fear? resentment? trauma? depression? grief? frustration? unfulfillment?
- And then drop the label, the name of the emotion, and allow the emotion to simply *arise as nameless sensations*
- *They are history sensations of a history body of a historical story*
- Even if they are happening now or the situations are happening now, see them as repetitive history, of that which can dissolve this instant, no matter how "long" it's been there
- *Take history and time out of the emotion or sensation and allow it to be present here now, and dissolve here now*
- *Yet have no need for it to dissolve,* simply sit with it, as Presence, open and free, without suppressing it, and without contracting around it... stay open and let it be and flow
- *Allow that which is fresh and new... Presence... to be that which you Are*
- *And that fresh, radiant Presence exists as You here now*
- And allow historical content and emotion to now be story-free, commentary-free sensations, met with love

- Take out their past meanings
- Be not concerned with how the emotion got there; simply be with the energetic charge and allow it to soften and fade
- Welcome tensions or contractions around *wanting a daddy*
- Imagine the contraction expand as light and peace
- When any emotion/sensation flows to release, the *natural happiness-peace* already there beneath it, simply rises
- That *happiness-peace* is right here now, as the true essence of you
- Thoughts, emotions, persons, situations all change
- Give attention to that which does not change... Eternal Father Love, Light
- Rest as the *changeless* peace, love, happiness of *Divine Union... here in every instant*
- It is very, very subtle... be very still inside... abide in the sanctuary of stillness
- Then the subtle arises as ineffably potent
- In unlayering emotional storage, release thoughts of father and father story—allow the emotions to be storyless little movements, arising upon that which does not move or change
- *I Exist as Spirit Presence, one with Eternal Father*... the sensations of wanting a daddy melt into that
- In the "*I Exist as Spirit Presence, Eternal Father Love,*" all sense of any lack or want now fades into that *Eternal Love*, like shadows disappearing *into Light*
- Being one with *Father Ahavah Light,* lack disappears...

- Be aware of that which is subtle, changeless—immense *Eternal Spirit Father*, this instant, as the ground of being, the foundation...
- Take a moment to more and more deeply fall back into this
- Abide as *Father Ahavah Presence*

***

Feel self-compassion. You may sense love well up from "within," from a deep quiet place, or you may feel it as *Peace and Grace* that seems to descend upon you, and surround you as God Presence. Either way, feel this *Divine Father Love, this Spirit Presence, as you,* the most pure high clear reality of you.

Allow the *I want a Daddy so badly*—the feeling of lack of father, or absence of the masculine, to be nameless sensation, let go. And feel this *Father Spirit Love*, endless and eternal, strong and supportive, overflowing from spiritual resource within the heart.

Realize: *If I exist at all, and I do, I exist as Spirit. Spirit is beyond masculine and feminine, yet has the essence of each, in balanced completion.*

Rest in: *I exist as one with Father Ahavah, happening on the 'inside", as the core of being. No absence of love can occur in this reality.*

Have awareness that the *I want a Daddy so badly,* reflects the suppressed riveting ache for reunion with *Original Father.* Yet, we cannot have a genuine, honest absence of what we already are and have. *Lack:* a counterfeit, appearing so real. *Wanting:* an imposter state, requiring maintenance by struggle and effort.

Stress management equates to managing the duress of lack. We tolerate this stress management way of life without truly examining its source. Rather than manage stress, find it's true source. Lack feeds a false state of a "me," a false experiencer that seems to override the subtle infinite blessings ready to overflow.

Beneath the experience of lack lies the identity as the *experiencer*.

That's the true key: not the experience, the *identification as the experiencer*. Look beneath the experience: who is this *experiencer* of lack? Who is this person that wants? Refrain from answering that mentally. *Be very, very still.* Ask the question, from deeper than the mind chatter, deeper than the emotions, and then let the question go. Rest as Presence. In the Light of Presence, this *experiencer* of suffering is seen through. See through, move beyond, this *experiencer*.

The *experiencer* has filters.

Direct union with Presence, has no filters. Direct, face to face... with Eternal Love.

This Eternal Love is free of the pseudo experiencer chirping about experience...

Rather than asking *why is this missing? how come I don't have this? why did this happen again?*, ask who is this *false experiencer*, this *me*? Is this the truth of what I am? Original, in the beginning, Light, The Creator, does not lack, or want, or seek.

In the wanting a daddy, a father, the masculine... or wanting anything—a partner, an open door of contribution, affluence—beneath it lies a wanting of *Divine Love*.

That which you exist as is beyond a changing state. It is changeless *Being*, which is freedom, sacredness, preciousness, serenity, beauty.

Allow the *I want a daddy* sensations of lack, that longing for the sweet innocence of the father bond, to surface and disappear into pure light. And realize, I am one with the *Eternal Father* before all fathers.

Alive as adoration... Father Ahavah!

Selah!

Chapter Fourteen

The Power of Dissolving the Polarity

The highest, most sublime spiritual expansion occurs from dissolving the polarities around any pair of opposites.

As you shift back and forth between any two polarities, collapse into that which is beneath them or beyond them.

For example, in a rejection vs. validation polarity, either pole of these two opposites can be released into the *Spirit Presence* beneath them. In releasing the polarity of health vs. illness, both concepts of feeling vitality vs. feeling depleted fade into the underlying *Eternal Life*. And that life then expresses as spirited wellbeing.

Beneath or beyond the polarity of human love vs. human hate exists the *True Love, Divine Love, Spirit Love* that does not change.

Beneath or beyond the polarity of poverty vs. wealth exists the *Infinite Spirit* of boundless resource—*God as Source,* yet in a way of intimate union.

The spiritual wisdom of polarity release offers a powerful key to freedom from father wounds. The whole experience of feeling "lacking masculine love" vs. "having masculine love" occurs only at one level of experience. However, realization of being one with, *of being, Father Ahavah Presence, rests beneath, above and beyond both of those.*

Instead of trying to "solve the problem" by somehow gaining masculine love or compensating for the perceived lack in other ways, we shift our identity. It is beyond an identity shift from wounded daughter to fulfilled woman, or one *who longs* for fathering to one *fulfilled* in father love. It is an identity shift from personal "me" to *Eternal Spirit*.

It is an identity shift from mortal, limited, mental-emotional personality, to infinite, immortal, *God Being, Presence.*

Here, we look at how to release each side of the polarity and rest into (rest as) the *Spirit Presence, Eternal Light,* "beneath" or "beyond" that duality or polarity.

With suffering, with thoughts, beliefs, emotions—realize these happen on a surface and changing level. At the core, we exist as changeless sacred Spirit, before or beyond any opposites, dualities, or polarities.

Take a moment to feel this vital key awareness. *Oneness with God Spirit is ineffable peace, happiness, holiness,* before the *belief* in any pole of a polarity, or any pair of an opposite.

Have awareness of Father God as whatever name has the feeling of warmth and affection, such as *Abba Father, Papa Dios, Father God, or Divine Father.* Connect in a union with this *Eternal Father.* Know this as *Home, as the Original, Primordial Light, Supreme Creator.* Whatever name that we give, realize that the supreme

Holy One is beyond all names. In the ineffable resplendent speechless awe, the holiness, the Light, feels too sacred for any name. We have our closest approximations for names, the closest languaging we can offer for that which unravels us, redeems us, awakens us, as the beauty of holiness. It is ageless, timeless, nameless, before all time, before any ages, prior to the named.

We already exist as one with this *Nameless Holy Perfection, the Holy One, Eternal Father.*

Let go of consciously or unconsciously seeking a divine father connection. There is nothing to seek. All divine love is present, as *Presence,* this instant.

No seeking.

Allow all seeking of any kind to soften, fade, and disappear. Relax from seeking this *Divine Primordial Love* in anyone or anything, in anything named or external. There is nothing lacking or missing, nothing to pursue, go after, or newly attain. Release grasping or getting and *abide as the eternal emptiness.* Empty of focus on personal "me", sit as holy Oneness and behold the fruition—the kingdom of eternal harmony. This is not passive. Attentively blaze as this *Spirit Light,* and directly act when prompted by (as) *It.*

Open to feel this ecstatic joyful union, as *here now.* Discover the miraculous, exquisite, simple beauty of its subtleness.

The subtle is the essential.

The noisiness is the non-essential.

Rest as Presence. Contemplate the existence of this *Eternal Father,* as present here now, as one with you and as you.

Place, *deep, soft attention* on that peaceful contemplation *Father Ahavah*, then let go and relax, as if falling into the gap between thoughts, the gap between feelings. "Fall back" into the *Prior To Self* - prior to this world and its polarities, its uncertainties, and its hells.

Contemplate: "*Still Home, Father Love Presence, Prior To* earth father, *Prior To* thoughts, *Prior To* emotions, *Prior To* sensations, *Prior To* a conditioned, limiting self, *Prior To* this world, *Prior To* fear, *Prior To* the belief in death, *Prior To* the fear of death."

Rest as the deep stillness that remembers *Home,* and arises as *Home Presence, Prior To* any sense of separation.

Contemplate, and rest as if floating in a vast ocean of love and peace. Contemplate spiritual principle, and then release the contemplation and rest as silence. Feel the subtle, yet potent love right here now.

Experiential Application:

Polarity Process

- Allow the breath to be slow, full, deep
- Feel a rhythmic balance within the breath
- Have awareness of the breath, and have a circular breath, with no pause between the top of the inhale and as it flows into the exhale; or on the bottom of the exhale as it flows into the next inhale... for several breaths
- Relax the forehead muscles
- Soften the face and relax the jaw.... relax the shoulders
- Scan the body and notice any places of contraction and tension
- Feel these places open and relax, as if expanding the contraction to the space around you
- Imagine that your head has no borders, as if expanding it to the space in front of you, the right side expanding to the space, the left side to the space, the back of the head to the space
- Slowly move down the body, imagining expanding it to the space around you
- Imagine the body as filled with flowing golden light, that expands out all around the body, as if a column of light or a cocoon of light

- Allow thoughts to quiet by having little interest in the flow of thoughts
- See thoughts as part of a thought sphere, a streaming content, not even your most true thoughts
- Let thoughts be as a river that you do not have to know where it starts, or where it is going or where it ends... you watch the river, yet it's in the background, not the foreground
- Softly focus on *Spirit Presence* as the foreground... *Father Ahavah* as the foreground
- Attentive to this, immersed in this, being this... not following the neurochemical pull of thoughts, emotions sensations, circumstances
- Notice any sensation of "lack of father" (or the masculine love, nurture, support) and the accompanying experience of sadness, anxiety, withdrawal, resentment...
- Notice any sensation of *lack of family* or *longing for family* or longing for a more complete, intimate, honoring experience of family or partnership
- Feel these now as storyless sensations, the raw, unfiltered emotion, and let go and release
- Open to release the deepest core root of longing for closer father love, or masculine validation
- Welcome, embrace, and release these feelings of the "bad" side of the polarity (father absence or father abuse)
- Step back and observe beliefs and emotions—not indulging them or escaping them—face them from a step back... allow them to melt into love... open the heart and let go

- Rest as the open space for these experiences to rise, to be welcomed into love, and to dissolve into this open space of peace
- As you release this "side" of the polarity, fall back into that which is beneath it
- Rest as the "inner" *Father Ahavah Presence*, happening beneath or beyond physicality
- Next, have awareness of wanting, or of having the opposite polarity—"good" father experience, or the "good" masculine attentive caring
- Imagine being the apple of your father's eye and having a kind, warm, affectionate experience (if not your father, imagine any masculine figure)… notice and soften inner resistances that arise
- You may also imagine this as a nameless, faceless image—a father figure you imagine as close, benevolent, wise, bestowing
- And then release any thought of that, desire for that, apathy toward that, or happy feelings of that… be neutral toward that… more interested in *Father Ahavah*…
- Thus release the "good" side of the polarity, going deeper than and beyond that
- And rest in the "inner" love presence, *Spirit Presence*, beneath and beyond that
- Notice that the highest freedom means not being attached to or focused on either side of the opposite poles… true peace comes from resting as the *Presence of Love* within, being the *Eternal Father Presence*, and allowing that to "form" in whatever way it forms

- Have awareness again of the polarity side of the "bad" dad, the "negative" experience or absence or lack of masculine love or nurture, no matter how intense or how mild it feels
- Welcome the feelings, thoughts, beliefs, as sensations, and "sit with them" not needing to jump out of them
- Not "sitting on" to suppress them... "sitting with" to allow them to rise and fade
- And feel them fade to background in the softly blazing Light of *Eternal Papa Presence*
- Rest as that which is changeless, beneath or prior to, pairs of opposites polarity
- Then again, imagine a dad or father figure as benevolent, honoring
- Release the "good" side of the human father experience
- Rest as that formless *Divine Papa, Eternal Father Presence*, that can form or not form and it doesn't matter which, because this *Love* means more than anything else
- Realize that this *Presence* —beyond or beneath either side of a polarity— is the true freedom
- Practice more "rounds" of feeling and releasing the "bad" or "negative" father or masculine wounding—resting as the *Father Ahavah* beneath and beyond; and then feeling and releasing the "good" or "wanted" father or masculine, rest in *Father Ahavah* beneath and beyond that
- Go back and forth between the polarities until the *Father Ahavah* is the only interest and the deep, abiding experience... the stable, secure, changeless *Father Ahavah*

- Feel free from the inner movement and constant changes of ego... the subtle movement from *I don't want that*, to *I do want this*
- Discover how that little movement keeps a personal "me" identity maintained, and a survival focus going—this is a huge key
- Allow identification and awareness to shift to *that which does not move and does not change, the subtle pure presence:* "I Am That"
- And then Rest as: "*I AM*"
- Have awareness of "*I AM*," Eternal, Holy Sacredness
- Go back and forth between the polarities as many times as you wish, speeding up the time between them until the polarities collapse into *Presence*
- That which you are is free, this instant
- As *Eternal Father Ahavah*

Selah!

Chapter Fifteen

Wake Up!
The Dream-Like Movie

All suffering, at its core, is existential suffering. Meaning: We forgot.

We forgot that we exist as *One with God*.

We exist as the entirety of *God Life, Spirit Presence;* unconditional tenderness. Creator God is Eternal. Eternal means unchanging and permanent.

The highest wisdom defines the *real* as that which is *permanent*.

Pause for a moment to see the key of *permanence*: that which does not change, is that which *Is Real*.

The changeless Presence is that which is Real.

Adore the *Real*.

This understanding goes beyond thinking, learning or reading. Go deeper; allow the contemplation of your real being to spark a remembrance of changeless real *Father Ahavah*, and rest in that.

The world we sense with our physical senses—what we hear, see, taste, touch, and smell—is not permanent.

And the thoughts and emotions, which arise from these sensations, change. Thus, day-by-day… hour-by-hour… moment-by-moment, situations and our perceptions about them change.

Emotions change.

Thoughts change.

Thoughts, emotions, and circumstances are not as tangible, actual, or solid as we think; they are fluid.

Our identification with the three-dimensional world is like watching scenes on the mind's screen, similar to a movie or last night's dream.

We cannot understand higher awareness, or Divine Union, as a mental concept—like we memorized multiplication tables in grade school. We first open to the seed of truth. Then we behold it watered with contemplation and blossomed with surrendered emptying of all else. *Divine Grace,* the anointing of *Presence* then awakens the pinnacle of direct experience, the zenith of calm ecstatic joy.

Just as a thought from a moment ago is not here now, each passing moment is not "here" now in a permanent way. Almost as fast as you experience that moment, it has *passed*, become *the past*, the way one frame on a reel of film passes, as the next image comes up for view.

Know reality, non-dream as Presence.

It Is Original Self.

Real.

Not the fake self.

Eternal Presence, Is… total completion… no lack.

Live as One with *That*.

Any other identity… is… dying… walking toward dying…

Turn around.

Wake up and live.

I Am That, Prior To the character, movie, or dream of separation.

We dream a dream, construct a cinema show, of being limited, powerless, and separate, yet all the while, we are one with the *Infinite Life of God Presence.*

Infinite does not mean a greater quantity of "finiteness." It means not finite.

Open this gift of surrender and mastery. Spiritual adepts, sages, and saints know this as *moving through the eye of the needle*. Wake up! As Light! in this *context* of this world—the world of duality, of suffering.

We live as that One Holy Presence, while seeming to walk in full functioning radiance of vital life in this world.

When we are aware of physical form and yet more identified as *Spirit Light*, forms tend to reflect that essence of *Light*, harmony, and beauty. Yet, when we identify and focus more on mental/emotional, conditioned states, then the physical experiences and physicality may reflect those states. Therefore, geographical, relationship, or financial states may mirror the repressed emotional pain, or inner convictions.

We could perceive mental-emotional states and life circumstances, as having a dream-like quality—like film images, movie images, still frame images, flowing in such rapid succession that they appear as a cohesive story. To feel separate from God Presence... is a dream-like anesthetized state. To feel suffering... is a dream-like state. To imagine we die... is a dream-like state. To feel limited and lacking... is a dream-like state.

Knowing this does not make us irresponsible, uncaring or unproductive. Knowing this isn't an excuse to *flake* on people and on life. Truly experiencing the deepest realizations of this dream-like quality, allows us to "function" with the highest intelligence, depths of love, radiant presence, and creative mastery. We see all beings and events as sacred. We stay present and active in the messy situations and painful moments. *We still show up.* We see through the fleeting dream-like mirages, and live anchored in the reality of *Father Ahavah, Eternal God.*

Clarity about the transitory nature of the sensory world allows less survival-based reaction, and more depth of compassion. We deal actively and directly with life, as if it were truly solid, and real. Our true ground of being illumines as more potent Light, revealing the sensory perceptions as a more superficial level.

This is the true ascendant forgiveness: seeing through the dream-like quality of passing events. Otherwise we live with a belief of "he" or "she" or "life" did this to "me." Even if we feel that way initially, or a situation calls for decisive actions or consequences for others behaviors, step back and rest. Remember the Eternal

Reality, and zoom out for the wider, grander view. From this height, graciousness allows the most disheartening of situations to appear as a speck of dust in the golden kingdom of *You*.

As the vital totality, *Spirit Reality*, we see this world as more shadowy, more temporal. And we see on some level, this is "my" dream-like movie. Yet now we see through the concepts, conditioning, limitations, separate "me" that it creates.

It is not just the traumas or trials of life that arise as this dream state, but also the seemingly "good" experiences!

We wish to rise in awareness beyond the "good" and "bad" polarities and pairs of opposites, to exist as the Eternal Reality.

It is not the images (persons, situations, circumstances, dramas) that arise on the screen of the life movie that are most significant. It is our response to them.

Where are we looking from, and what we are looking out as? The key is our response, and what we identify as. The situation fades and passes, the same way temporal movie screen image does. Identity as Spirit, does not fade and pass, it a*rises as eternality.*

Pause for a moment, as if leisurely drinking in the fragrance of a plumeria flower, and rest in the perfume of its beauty and peace. Pause as if looking at a pearl, and seeing all its subtle variations of soft color and light. Stop now, and open to feel the perfume of peace, the illuminating pearls of joy, in the realization that *what we exist As, as already Home as Spirit Light,* is the key—not what occurs in the events of life or the thoughts or emotions of reaction to the movie.

Our divine response means our directly experienced point of identification. Our ultimate response is our *identification as One with the ineffable Holy One.*

We know how contracted and limiting it feels to respond as mental/emotional reaction, as personal "me," stuck at that reference point. Now we see how expansive and limitless it feels to release mental/emotional reaction, see through beliefs and concepts, see beyond circumstances, and remember self as *Essential Self, Spirit Self. The Prior To Self,* that needs no reference points - I Am Alive as One with that, It lives here.

This identification lifts us from the belief in and attachment to the dream-like state of movie-like scenes. We see it, feel it, sense it, respond to it, yet we are not plugged into it, over-run by it, invested in it.

We have a new treasure and eternal investment—the heart's true *Home.*

We no longer have to pay the mortgage of unhappiness, believing a dream-like temporary cinema. We remember *Home*—free, open, spacious happiness.

We still function in the world, often with more effective and radiant service and power for goodness. Overflowing fruition visibly unfolds, and life shines as "heaven on earth."

Seeing through the dream-like movie requires the undoing of seeking and wanting. Pause now and notice any subtle mental or emotional movement of "I don't want this."

Take a few slow deep breaths, open to new clarity and see the counter-movement of "I do want this." Although it may seem like a step up to move from "I don't want… (separation, aloneness, poverty, lack, limitation, disease)" to "I do want… (solidarity, communion, affluence, givingness, health, vitality)," it represents a lateral movement… going nowhere.

The most clean, joyful liberation occurs through releasing both sides of the polarity.

Softly Be God Presence, that has no "want"—no belief in, or concept, or feeling of, or experience of "want."

Feel the stillness of not wanting. There is only this instant; open to this instant being complete. *Softly, Silently Be…* without the movement of being—or not being—this or that.

The dawning of remembrance that "I exist as God Presence" is the beginning of heaven. Yet, in beginning, in the original beginning, we were created as that light of heaven, and we still exist as that, effortlessly, here now.

"I am a person and I do not want that and I do want this" is the little movement that starts the spiral down into the agony of lack.

As soon as we wish it to be different, this moment is not complete, and we are in a psychological and existential hell. The emotional charge intensifies, the thoughts fire up, the mind commentary chirps up, the suffering increases.

Right in this moment, stop and notice… and then release "I don't want this."

Feel into the resistance of "don't" and allow that energy to fade into nothingness. Beyond a mental concept of "don't" or don't want to feel the energy of it, the contraction of it. See how that energy is there all the time! Running life!

Alive as Presence, One with God Presence, the potency of that Light will unwind and dissolve this contracted energy of "don't." Notice any variations of "don't want" such as "this is awful," "hate this," "it never changes," "hope it changes in the future."

Pause now, and take a moment to identify the signature—the distinct *feeling* of "want," of "lack,"—and allow it to fade to neutral, and then to nothing. Realize the distinct difference between *"want"* versus *"have"* versus *"am."* For example observe the difference between *wanting* love, versus the essence of *having* love, or *being* love. Being the reality of love is real, is permanent, is non-dream. Wanting love is of the fabric of impermanent, changing, dream.

Feel the contraction, the heaviness around "I don't want this." And simply let it go like a hot potato. Drop it totally. Don't try to figure it out or defend it. Free of analyzing it —feel for the distinct feelingness of it and then open the heart to the *Love* that dissolves it. Rest as self-completion in this instant.

Rather than being a person who wants or doesn't want, be the *Presence that Is*, and that endlessly gives.

Rested as Being, we no longer avoid what arises in this moment. Beholding as *Light, as Self-Complete Presence*—we no longer feel a need to grasp, grapple, gratify.

Peace Is.

Be the *One, the Light, the Spirit Spaciousness* upon which the images, persons, situations, and thoughts rise and fall.

Be the watcher.

Then *watch the watcher.*

Spirit Aware of Spirit.

One with God Presence Prior To...

Be that Prior To Self, Prior To daddy, *Prior To* parents, *Prior To* the separate self identity, *Prior To* a personal "me," *Prior To* pain or suffering, *Prior To* any want or lack, *Prior To* this world, *Prior To* the watcher of this world.

Open to innately feel that the watcher and what is watched, reflect this same Light as its core essence.

Realize existence as infinity, as eternality, as limitless.

Before we felt fear... want... reaction... stress... that now fades into emptiness. We now know emptiness as aliveness, as *Spirit Life*, so potent that all else appears to it, rises and falls upon it, and reflects the light essence of it.

Ask, am I the content of "my life" or the one to whom it appears?

Ask, *Who Am I?* Yet realize there is no mental answer, there is no name, person, personality that defines that. *Who Am I?*

Ask, who is the one that suffers? Asking this—without thinking, unknowing—reveals that this personality "self" does not have the solid permanent existence we thought it did.

Moving beyond the fears of that, emptied of personal-self attachments, we know *Self —as one with God Presence*, as Holiness Bliss, as Eternal Happiness.

Unwinding the emotional charge of "wanting" and "worrying", alive as adoration, as *Light*, the mere thought of a beautiful, harmonious happening, and it may effortlessly happen.

We remember how to create as we were designed to create—which is to behold. In the natural way, the original way, a mere illumined divine thought of something and it appears as light form, as formation. Divine thought has a more rarefied, impersonal, feeling, such as an impulse, an essence. This differs from the human thought stream of repetitive opinions, judgments, fears, conditioning, attributed meanings, and want.

Rather than effort, trying, or struggle… *we behold.*

Rather than creating, we receive the impulse, the inspiration, and step back and *behold.*

We tangibly, potently exist as the glory of God—the sweet, rich totality of paradise, of heaven. And we *behold* it miraculously unfolding as our earth experience.

Scripture states, "The kingdom of God is within you." It is within—not something without that you want, seek and attain.

Scripture does not state that the kingdom of God *will be* within you… at some future time. It *is* within you.

Now.

Is means *Now.*

Eternal Life Is Now… and "continues" after the dream-like cinema, after the incarnation, after this persona no longer appears in third-dimensional time-space life span.

When we see through the temporary life span movie, the fear of death (that underlies all other fears) dissolves. We wake up now, not after death, as the eternal life that is one with *God Presence*, in profound peace and true erasure of fears and stress.

We exist beyond being the "son" or "daughter" of anyone or anything finite or limited. We have life as the offspring of Father God, of Mother God; and we exist as Oneness with that Original Supreme Creator, before gender qualities. We could say, at one level, we exist as the genderless offspring of the genderless *Eternal One*. *We exist as one with the Eternal God Light,* which is *Prior To* gender, yet can express as gender.

As we remember that, sacredness comes alive. This innate luminous worship shines, and nothing of this world—of this world of the dream of separation can add to or take away from that.

Rest deeply… cherished… cherishing.

Rest in the trustworthy embrace, the loving gaze, of the *Father Ahavah. The Real.*

Feel the ecstatic calm of humility, the *Holy Emptiness, the Immortal Freeing,* and behold that form as all limitless beauty, and all infinite creation.

Once in meditation an insight arose: "Make all the slides the same." Pause the movie to "still frame," and make all of them the same. A calm joy arose in the felt *Presence* of profound stillness, eternal freedom.

We could see this world and the life journey as similar to a high technological theatre. Imagine purchasing a movie ticket and siting in a velvet seat in a darkened movie theater, with hot popcorn and epic technology. Pretend you sync up with an apparatus that allows you to actually feel the sensations of the protagonist in the movie. When the main character feels the wind rush across the face, you feel it. When they walk, you feel your legs in motion. When they cry, you feel a wave of sadness and tears well up behind your eyes. When they pet their dog, you feel the sensation of the palms of your hand stroking fur.

Imagine when the star of the movie perceives identity like a body-mind personality separate from Spirit life, you feel like a personal "me" in survival. It has a sticky, entangled, emotionally charged feeling. When they think a thought, you think that thought. When they contract or feel fear, you feel it. When they cook dinner, you seem to move, stirring vegetables and mashing the potatoes.

Thus, in this scenario you see the body-mind-emotion experience as a movie, a play, an imagined essence that feels real, just like last night's dream seems real until you wake up. Yet, it's temporary and has no lasting life or truth in the core of being.

What you exist as in reality is that which does not change. *Identify as that: Changeless. What is here now, as Now, that does not change?*

It's all in the stillness, the silence, the subtlety. And it's all in the passion to realize divinity. This becomes so potent that a critical mass shift occurs, the realization dawns, *I AM that Spirit*. And yet even the *I Am Spirit* fades away as empty nothingness, as you rest as that beyond words or thoughts. And yet that nothingness is the Light of holiness that is the *All*.

Open to have an awareness, even if not yet a deep understanding, simply an initial awareness, or a beginning of curiosity: "what if this were like a dream?"

What if when I woke up from a dream, I realized, *I am awake now; my dream did not occur?* What if no one really wakes up; the person that seems to wake up is not true identity in the first place. God Presence is, as the real, and that felt reality is known as self.

Be *the Spirit Presence, Still Home, awake to* the movie. Be the *One* aware of the dream-like temporary character, the emotions, the thoughts, the circumstances.

Rest as awake awareness. In that way, "redeem" the dream. You resurrect the images that appear as physical life. You move beyond past, beyond limitations, beyond beliefs, to the *Spirit Life* which is fresh, new, bright, open paradise.

That which you are is fresh this instant, free this moment. Be suspicious of any experience unfolding as stuck, unremitting, tiring, cyclical. It's the repetitive slides replaying as the dreamy cinema of *belief... of separation.*

Abide as the spontaneous, essential Spirit Presence.

And then watch the "dream" movie reflect more of the gardens of heaven, as simple, clean utopia. However, the true miracle is peace within, regardless of what happens in the movie of life. At times the rugs get pulled out, or what we built for years crumbles, or relationships seem to break apart, or a life career ends. These may trigger unconscious fears, beliefs, and emotions, providing rich opportunity to release limiting self-perceptions, forever.

Thus, we cannot determine "good" or "bad." Whatever happens, meet changes from the place within that knows the eternal ground of being.

If trials, tribulations, suffering or pain arise, meet them with a deeper *Presence*. A new surrender, a deeper insight, a fresh awareness, dawns. At times the more impossible a situation seems, the deeper you must surrender into the awareness of being *Presence*. Rather than a person with a problem, or one stuck in suffering, realization dawns of being *Presence,* being the timeless Principle (of love, harmony, completion, peace, fulfillment).

Miraculous Grace occurs in the peace felt within. Yet inner and outer are not seen as two, they are seen more as Light, reflecting harmony.

Often the greatest miracle is the simple, open Life in this moment. At times the true miracle involves emptying attachments and dissolving rigid opinions. It is releasing the past, the future, the outcome, the situation, and being the exquisite, stillness of *Presence* here now.

And then life unfolds as spontaneous fulfillment, like the *Natural Self*.

The reference point of self: *Light aware of Light*.

In this instant, you exist as free, *Eternal Light*, in the timeless now of reality.

Father Ahavah!

Selah!

Chapter Sixteen

Embracing

Prior to Daddy: The Feminine Light
Prior to the Feminine Light: Father Ahavah

We live in a culture that often defines happiness as attaining pleasure and avoiding pain.

Yet, nothing can truly be escaped or avoided. Nothing needs to be sidestepped or negated. And true causeless happiness has nothing to do with temporary transient sensations of pleasure.

Father pain… daughter wounding… being unfathered… son wounding… the ache for spiritual fathering… cannot be suppressed, glossed over or dismissed with a thought. When it is fully owned, totally embraced, and deeply felt, then it can be authentically released, deeply dis-identified with.

In spiritual growth, pain with "father" or "the masculine" situations or memories may initially intensify. Be kind to yourself in this process. Yet, do not indulge in or make it a drama. Face the pain, the loss, and radically surrender to Divine Grace on the deepest levels.

I discovered that as the pain from abuse unwound, from the psyche, thoughts, beliefs, and emotions—and as the spiritual wisdom revealed this as impersonal, not happening to a person (as she was no longer the primary identity)—an unexpected phenomenon occurred.

This may not occur with others; each will have their own process.

The global pain of father/masculine abuse coursed through my whole being and body, yet "I" was not personally identified with it—I was the open field of the Light of compassion—and surrendered as Presence. It was a witnessing and carrying of "the pain," the midwifing of the collective pain, of the dishonor of the feminine.

This tsunami of global pain was intimately felt, with deep compassion, and Divine Love engulfed it.

Rather than abuse happening to a "me," the global dynamic of "the pain" was allowed to move through the *Spirit Reality* and collapse into nothingness. It took immense dedication and focus to hold the tension for that alchemical transmutation.

For a time, it was a pole-to-pole, back and forth shift—first, in one instant, feeling the global pain, and then in the next moment, almost simultaneously, feeling the most potent intimate Divine Love and ecstatic holy joy. And then the instants collapsed together—embraced in *Father Ahavah* Divine Love, while simultaneously feeling the feminine and masculine collective pain evaporate in the Light of this Love.

There is tremendous power and exquisite grace in making this conscious: 1) the personal "me" welcomes and releases thought and emotion as mere arisings, then 2) centering beyond identity as a "me" to the realization of identity as *Presence,* then 3) aware of the personal self and world, from *Presence.*

Embrace Presence.

Abide as the Light.

Embracing and abiding—by *not* returning to a personal "me" identity, rather going back prior to, and beyond, to the reality.

The mind cannot grasp or do this at a mental level.

This occurs by having the intention and awareness, and surrendering to Grace. It is experienced at first in glimpses, then as the strength of mastery.

The human mind has to know—it has to be firmly instructed and informed—that it does not have the permanent answers to suffering. Appealing to the human mind thought stream for our ultimate spiritual answers is like going to a child in kindergarten to solve a trigonometry problem. Imagine doing that every moment, every hour, every day for years—to finally discover that the answer will not ever arrive from there. The mind does not know; it cannot find the way. The mind constitutes a repetitive, conditioned, yet "innocent" hindrance. We do not have to see the mind as "bad." However, we often bow to it as a wild stallion of power that drags us in the dust behind it. We are to master the horse of the mind, calm and tame it. Scripture refers to this as "set your mind on things above, not on earthly things." We set the mind moment by moment. Is it set on the world and repetitive "me" thoughts, or is it set on the above, Divine Presence? Live from the heart, spirit, and allow that to govern the mind.

The human mind is useful for some practical matters, like balancing the checkbook or the choosing to drink filtered water in a crystal glass rather than stagnant water from a muddy birdbath. The human mind has use for stopping at a red light or writing out a phone message.

Actually though, in highest spiritual flow of awareness, even those things simply occur naturally, automatically, without needing the mind.

Nonetheless, we credit the human mind with functionality in daily life activities. However, know that the mind does not have the answers to suffering, or to spiritual life, or to love, eternality, miracles, or limitlessness.

For *that*, drop down into the *Heart*.

Open the whole being to feel, know and remember God Presence, to remember the infinite, the limitless and the love that is true love.

The mind does not have the answer to the global pain, to the collective suffering. Only being *Home*, in the Heart of God does.

Divine loving union with *Holy Light* does.

Aliveness as *Father Ahavah*, does.

Experiential Application:

Prior To Daddy

Father Ahavah

- Settle into a comfortable position, where you are relaxed, yet attentive
- Take a few slow, deep, full, breaths
- Breathe deeply in slow, circular breaths
- Allow the thoughts to slow and the mind to quiet, simply by placing attention on the breath for a moment
- Slowly scan your body, part by part, and pause to relax at any point of tension or contraction... take a couple of minutes for this
- Contemplate: "set not your mind on things of the earth, set your heart on things above"
- Open to a deeper awareness of not setting the mind on the earth—what you see, hear, touch, taste or smell...
- You can interact with—and love and bless—things of the earth without setting the heart upon them as if they are your life or your answer
- With eyes open, look upon an object in the room
- Notice how you may have "gone out" to the object, or become immersed in it, or you "moved out" toward it
- Now notice the same object without going out to the object

- You can "have" the object, "experience" the object without depending upon it for happiness, or avoiding it if you feel aversion, or getting lost in it
- Stay focused, fully present, with the totality of self here as Presence
- Remain aware of the object—without moving toward it
- Stay present and observe—looking factually at lines and shapes and colors
- Pause to notice this huge key to *being in the world, yet not of it*, or abiding in *Eternal Spirit* without attaching to the world that changes: *Look factually at objects as lines, shapes, and colors*
- Practice not giving objects a name: *simply lines, shapes, colors at a surface level*
- Now close eyes and imagine you see that object through closed eyes
- Open the eyes, and see that same object, looking out from the observing Love
- Have no need to name the object, see it as *simply shapes, lines, colors*
- Have no attachment to the object, no name, no meaning, simply *look*
- Notice the feeling of *clean simple looking*, without "going out to" the object, or attaching to the object, or making it more real than Spirit
- Pause and feel this... *Spirit Presence* more *real* than the object
- See that as a huge key!

- Close eyes, and imagine the same object through closed eyes
- Notice the difference between looking at an object (or person, or situation) and going out to it, as if hungrily grasping it... and looking neutrally, complete as *Spirit Presence*
- Now, practice this for a few rounds, or repetitions... on the inhale, eyes are open, observing the object while staying present, non-attached... and upon the exhale, close eyes and imagine seeing the same object... simple unnamed lines, shapes, colors
- Then after a few cycles of that, leave the eyes closed, except for when you need to read the next line of this practice before closing eyes again
- Rest as the *Observing Spirit Love* that sees... without needing anything from what it sees
- Again pause to notice a huge key: observing, as *Spirit*, not needing anything from what it sees, needing nothing from the world... being the Light of the world
- *Spirit ever is... beholds... gives*
- Allow the mind to quiet even more; thoughts now like a nearly inaudible radio in the next room... low volume background noise
- Have awareness of emotions and allow them to simply be as sensations, welcomed and let go
- Notice that thoughts, emotions, beliefs, arise as "this world"
- Yet, on a deeper level, you *know the Golden World* of the kingdom of heaven within

- And abiding as that... look... and no matter what you see... still abide as *The Light, The Life* that is more real than images that fade
- Expand out to the wider view of being *Happiness Spirit, Holiness Presence*
- Know this *Eternal Essential Self as* exquisitely unique, yet not personal, not squeezed into a me and mine
- Notice this impersonal freedom, ease, spaciousness...non-attachment to the world...
- Then rest even deeper than this, another step back, remember *Home... Original Light... Pure God Oneness*
- Rest deeper as the impersonal—yet intimate—*Spirit Life, and Light...*
- Contemplate: *Prior To, The Holy One Presence,* and completely relax in surrender as *Original Innocence...*
- Rest in the lap of *Father Ahavah... the Eternal Love Prior To all suffering*
- Embrace the Eternal Holy Spirit
- Abide in love union with and as That
- In that dropping back, that *Prior To,* there exists an exquisite stillpoint of total completion... an emptiness of suffering or conflict... ineffable silence...
- Feel the profound peace and the ecstatic, clean bliss of that emptiness
- Cling to nothing and to no one
- Let God be enough!
- Expand until you feel as if all the world could disappear and there you are... tenderly embraced as one with *Eternal Creator...* immense golden *Christed Love*

- Open for that emptiness of conditioning, surrender into and as *Presence, which may* form in every treasure, every miracle, yet no form is needed to *Be It*
- Rest as *Original God Light, Heart of Father Ahavah*
- Abide as *the Emptiness...* that is within all things as a spark of Light... free of seeking... clean, pure, empty... as *Clear Light*
- Rather than a daughter (or son) longing for father love or masculine honoring, I AM One with *Original Holiness Life, Adoration Light of Eternal Father,* upon which mortal daughter and father rises and falls back into *Immortal Light... Still Home*
- *Home in the Heart*
- *Home*
- *Father Ahavah!*

Selah!

Chapter Seventeen

The Power of Prior To

The only self that does not suffer is the *Prior To Self*.

The Prior To Self is: *Prior To* suffering, *Prior To* this world.

It is *Prior To* daddies, *Prior To* "good" father or "negative" father, *Prior To* "good" mother, or "negative" mother.

It is *Prior To* duality, *Prior To* opposites, *Prior To* pain, *Prior To* limitations, *Prior To* any perceived lack of any kind.

The Prior To Self is the Original Self in its Original Innocence.

It Is One.

It is Prior To duality.

It is total completion *Prior To* lack. *It is* total limitlessness, *Prior To* limitation.

It is the Emptiness Bliss from which any and all things can form in heaven-like, paradise-like formation.

And yet the Prior To Self welcomes and holds the space of love for all things (appearances of lack, limitation, loss, fear). It reveals the *Prior To* perfection, there as "underlying" Light, all the time.

The *Prior To Self,* is the seamless space, the *Eternal God Presence, the Pure Land,* before belief, before thought, before rejection, before harshness, before suffering, before seeking, before proving, before competing, before surviving.

The *Prior To Self is the simple, natural, essential essence, Self.* It is prior to illness, prior to the belief in death, prior to fatigue, prior to trauma, prior to abuse, prior to healing abuse, prior to making a mess, prior to cleaning up a mess, prior to any need or lack or want of any kind.

The *Prior to Self* is prior to "good" and prior to "bad". It is prior to "I don't want this" and it is prior to "I do want that". It is prior to the most subtle movement of trying to get by, prior to the most intense passionate cutting quest for survival.

The *Prior To Self, Father Ahavah,* is prior to desire.

The Prior to Self is prior to any and all fear. It is prior to the fear of death, which is the root of all fears. *The Prior to Self is the Eternal Life that never fears and that never dies.*

The Prior To Self is not burdened with trying to survive, or attain. It is not trying to avoid pain or attain pleasure. It is not trying to gain significance or "be somebody". It is also not trying to be "nobody" and withdraw and disappear.

The *Prior To Self* is timeless bliss, the stillpoint of peace, the emptiness that is empty of all things, yet is all things.

The *Prior to Self, is Oneness.* It is not attached to, diminished by, plugged into or limited by the world or world events or persons, or circumstances. It is not defined as a past or a future. It does not see any person or event as something to resist, or avoid.

The Prior To Self Is.

It seamlessly sees the world and all in it, without attaching to what is objective or seen. Yet it is *Presence as Love,* to and for all beings and things.

The *Prior to Self, Father Ahavah Self* is potent, unstoppable, immense Love.

It allows all things, all beings to rise upon this *Divine Love,* and remember and come *Home to this Eternal Love… as this Eternal Love.*

Welcome Home

Come Home

Home

Father Ahavah

Forever

Now

Selah!

Chapter Eighteen

Giving Birth: The Daughter of the Fire as the Heart of the Father

I had a partner who reflected my father.

The more I stepped into contribution and success, the more he criticized, invalidated and thwarted progress.

He was a master at shutting down my brightest moments.

No matter how I released, meditated, or processed, the pain intensified.

Miracles happened, and magnificent doors opened—rather than honoring and joining in that—his rejection turned to demoralizing cruelty.

He lacerated the sensitive places within that linked to the global empath within. *The abandonment of the feminine arose as an* the inner travail. The *Quieting* arose, calm and quiet, yet I felt a pressure of deep contractions around the heart.

I observed his wounded masculine, threatened by my expression of the masculine. Yet, he also resisted the feminine within me, and especially the *Light of the Divine Feminine*. The depth and potency of the *Divine* shining through, was too threatening.

Yet it was only revealing, reflecting to him, his true magnificence, what he truly is: divinity, limitlessness, beauty, mastery.

Rather than joining with that, he joined with the sabotage patterns, the dominance patterns, the familiar status quo patterns.

At a moment of the heart breaking open to the depths of compassion, I spoke about this to a dear friend and he said, "You're right there… you're ready to give birth to something, something is ready to be born."

Later, I sat by the ocean, watching the sparkling, dancing play of sunbeams on the blue green water.

I felt as an open, spacious radiance of *Original Light*, enveloping an ancient pain too deep for words, or for thoughts or prayers.

I asked "what is ready to be born, what is birthing?"

And I inwardly heard: *"The Daughter of the Fire, as the Heart of the Father. Father Ahavah—the profound, exquisite ineffable Divine Father Love."*

A soft message unfolded within:

As you are aware
No man can contain you

Or usher you in
Or midwife you
Or be the supreme reverence of the
Immensity of the Light

This Sacred Birth
No One Can Do
Or Help
Or Support
Or Contain
Or Facilitate

Resist Not Aloneness
Surrender In Being Totally Alone
Welcome Profoundly Alone
Stand Alone

The One Who is Alone
Set Apart
Merges Into
And As
The Divine God Light

In This Personal "me" Dissolution
Surrender Into
Alone
Profoundly Alone
Look to No One
In this Sacred Womb of True Life
True Life Aware of Itself

It's God Birthing Itself,

Extending Itself as You
Yet, You Now Remember That
As It Already Occurred
When Creator God
Light
Birthed You
As Light

Eternal Light
Remembering Itself as Eternal Light
Still Home
This Oneness of Eternal Light Now

The Daughter of the Fire
Stands in Total Completion
With No One
No Where
No Thing
And Rises as the Heart of the Father
With No One
No Where
No Thing
Yet the Daughter as the Heart of the Divine Father
Blesses, Loves, Is, All Beings, All Things

The Daughter of the Fire
The Innocence, Wonder,
Holiness, Sacredness, Miraculousness
Pure Clean Light
Ablaze as Feminine
One With Divine Mother
Yet as Daughter Fire

Mother Daughter Births Father Son
The Divine Masculine
Light, Love, Adoration

The Divine Feminine And Masculine
Unify
As The Holy Light

Daughter of the Fire
Birth the Heart of the Father
Alive as You

Yet Father Ahavah
Birthed The Daughters of Fire
And Sons of Fire
To Usher The Heart of the Father
In Every Point of Infinity
Including the Dot of Infinity
We Know as Earth

This Father Ahavah
Birthed Its Light
As the Daughters & Sons
Who Now Remember This Eternal Origin
And Birth This Heart of the Father
On Earth
And In All Hearts

Home

Father Ahavah!

Selah!

Chapter Nineteen

Pruning?
Or the Divine Shattering
Open In Light

There is a human, trauma shattering.

And there is a *Divine Shattering*.

They are worlds apart.

Yet, when we surrender the trauma shattering into the *Divine Shattering*, this opens the doorways of such rarefied reverence that the "self" emerges as *Immaculate Light*.

The message of this chapter does not describe anything that a person can do.

Or even engineer.

It is not on the level of psychology.

Or spiritual learning.

It is not of the mental, emotional, psychological, or situational realm.

It is a sacred rite of passage.

It spontaneously, suddenly, summons you to the radical surrender—a dying and resurrecting into *total trust* and *unstoppable glory.*

Something beyond this world, beyond human conditions, beyond personal strength, beyond mediocrity, orchestrates this narrow passageway through a black emptying void—that emerges as the golden pregnant *silence.*

A friend noticed a tender exquisite emptiness, and asked me to describe what had happened. I attempted to express in language, a phenomenon that no words adequately convey. The rest of this chapter describes that reply.

"An excavating soft humility arises, a christening of this sweet annihilation of the non-essential self. The heart pulses in awe, a breathtaking surrender of everything a person was, even on the most subtle levels. There is no reference point for who she thought she was, or what she may have wanted, needed, or desired. It opens as a liberating aliveness. Thought slow to profound quiet. There arise periods of no thoughts. *Total quiet.* Engulfed as an ocean of silence. Open trust. An ecstatic potent simplicity".

And I continued:

"I once perceived refining fires, or a crucible of growth, as something a "you" goes into and a "you" emerges more purified. Now direct experience reveals this highest, more definitive and final crucible as a refinement from which a "me" does not emerge at all. Maybe something else does. Maybe nothing emerges. It does not matter. And then... Light dawns. *Living Light Is.* The soft shattering of all concepts of a "personal me" now opens the most tender, wild, unalloyed, sacred immensity of beholding holiness, being holiness. This is far beyond pruning."

"In typical pruning, we gently snip a branch, or two, and leave the tree and its roots. In this *Sacred Shattering*, no amount of branch-by-branch pruning reaches the core. Only *face-to-face with the Divine* does that in a deep, final, way. The personal "me" has to first heal and then develop, before entering this crucible in a supremely constructive, rather than destructive way. Then the blinding effulgent Light does not render one unable to function in the world, rather it serves as a catalyst for immense service and extremely efficient productivity."

"The self may first develop through such things as: higher learning, friendship bonding, leaving or transforming non-supportive relationships, spiritual study, successful contribution, and financial stability. The wounded self heals and integrates into a rich full life. The esteem rises. Yet the deepest conditioning of traumas, of wounds, of disappointments—and ultimately the existential pain of feeling separate from Creator—a sensory identification as "me"... remains. The most buried remnants of abuse, trauma, attachment, fear... remains. No matter how much one releases and processes, the "me" mental-emotional persona... remains. "I am this body, this is "me" identity... remains. In the subtlety of this personal "me", the wings stay clipped from their highest flight into the limitless. Limitations... remain. And the most astounding radiance of devotion and holiness... remains untapped, like unmined gold. A purposeful disciplined, vibrant life unfolds... yet the most luminous God Union... remains elusive."

"If the spiritual awareness is high, the emotional growth work sufficient, the surrender into Divine Union deep and authentic enough—the Divine tender grace dawns—the being is ready for this loving *Divine Shattering*.

And...

Then...

Here is comes.

Here it is.

The Divine Shattering.

It is not the expression of this self in the world that goes away. In fact it often looks to the world like this is some super human who masterfully expresses high creativity, love, beauty and service. Yet the "person", the point of identification, shifts dramatically and radically. An irrevocable surrender of the personal sense of self reveals the pearl of great price: *"If I exist at all, and I do, I exist only as Spirit, as one with God Presence, as the Absolute Light."*

This *Divine Shattering* differs from the human shattering. The human shattering leaves a personal "me" potentially opening to the Divine Presence—longing for that which is higher and sweeter than suffering. It may arise as "this can't be God, how do I find God?" "I seek God. I wish to know truth, to know Light, to know what love truly is and feels like."

The human shattering often jump starts with an intensely painful life event: a loved one dies, a career suddenly ends, a spouse leaves, a life threatening illness looms. Or it happens through a long series of repetitive emotional hurts, wherein we hit a breaking point. The pain serves as a prod toward spiritual growth;

we cry out in our whole being for answers and transformation. However, once the crises passes, and enough Grace washes over the heart for relief and comfort, if that heart cry arose from roots too shallow, the human shattering loses sacred focus and dissipates. The human runs the risk of turning pruning into a concept, or a mild form of personal growth.

The mild version of pruning may still cut away destructive habits, support greater self honoring, shift surviving to thriving. The sense of separation from God lessens, and glimpses of union with God slowly heighten.

The human pruning goes down like a grand *lent*, giving up anything from hair gel to honey… forsaking swearing and sweets… casting off everything from a desire for revenge, to a doubt about one's worthiness.

In the human shattering, a "me" is *pared down* to be more of a transparency for God… in a comparatively mild way.

Anything… anything… will be let go of… and a spiritual discipline adopted… if just the "me" can stay as the prime mover identity.

The human shattering happens less invasively as if by choice. It turns into a psychological program that runs like this: I am this good person who does good things. I give up grains and sugars, and surrender selfishness and bad attitudes. I placate with a platitude when someone is unkind. I tell jokes if someone seems too tense. I don't drink or I have "a glass of wine" or "a social drink". I am working out, taking care of myself, eating right. I go to church, and I read the Bible and I help out at the charity.

Yet there is still a "me".

There is nothing wrong with those things. Some of them may serve well as supportive habits and an expression of goodness in the world. Yet, they likely have nothing to do with the *Divine Shattering*.

In the *Divine Shattering*, the pruning shears alchemize into potent blazing rays of intense Light. You as a symbolic tree being pruned, no longer offer a branch and then another branch of the self. You are suddenly pulled up by the very roots... shaken tenderly and wildly to the core... all the leaves fall off... you are chopped up into pieces of wood... and thrown into the loving fires. Initially it is excruciating. And then... quickly... sweetly, exquisitely, supremely... liberating.

I remember fearing the *Divine Shattering*. Now I see it as the most humbling, sacred trust. It arises as the most tender, wild, sweet, sacred immensity of holy beauty.

The Gift.

There is a knowing that nothing of the "you" that you knew is left.

It is ash.

Yet not in a way of destruction or loss. It is the ashes of the not-self, the embers of illusions.

Ash cannot be put back together.

That is its beauty and its gift.

From ash a phoenix can rise.

Or an angel.

Not a personal "me".

From the midst of ash, all Light may luminously, eternally, immortally shine.

From ash a diamond heart can cast rays of splendor and treasures of grace.

From ash, the Light that *Is*, softly blazes as that *Is*.

The reference point of the personality character self is gone.

It cannot reconnect to the imprinted patterns lived from before.

The *Divine Shattering* may initially feel volatile and intensely emotional. Then a breathtaking calm rises from a faint latency, to the pervading pulsing ground of being. An exquisite spiritual stabilization reveals itself in felt tangible experience.

Initially it feels like a benevolently deconstructing tornado of a force of light. It's momentarily terrifying, and then seen to be very, very, supremely calm and safe. It nurtures like the manna of tenderness. The nectar of tenderness prevails as it softly shatters ignorance and illusions. It cleanses, it removes, it levels, all not of its highest radiance. Simultaneously it spins cocoons of exquisitely rarefied love, as the resting places of the immortals awakened to the pure land's way of heaven's paradise.

That which is shattered is seen to have had no true eternal value.

The spiraling rushing winds unwind the personality self, while the cocoons of the nectar of divine love resurrect the remembrance of "I Am Light."

And *That Light* alone.

Yet to the world, it looks like the personality self comes alive with miraculous wisdom, knowingness, vitalness, and gifts.

Yet, the inner experience is that the character self is as surrendered as a piece of wood that so surrenders to the fire that it turns to ash. And the blazing fire is there where the wood used to be.

The "*I AM That*" arises.

And yet it seems more subtle than, *Prior To,* the *I Am* Spirit.

It feels prior to being-ness. *Pre I Am. Pre* beingness.

The *Original Self, Father Ahavah.*

The *Prior To* name and *Prior To* form self.

Made exactly in the Light image of Supreme Divinity, God Origin, before form... even before *I Am* form.

You arise as a treasure house of golden radiance.

The sacred rite seems to open some gate of heaven that was shut tight before. Now the gates open and lavishly pour rivers of sublime wisdom.

Open.

Simple.

Radical surrender.

Emptied.

So dead to all the non-essential.

Ablaze with all that is True Life.

This all happens in the invisible realms. And it shows forth visibly. The whole landscape of the physical life may change in great upheavals that then flow into new vistas and bright horizons. Or the external life may look the same in its relationships and routines, yet the inner experience of it is vastly more sweet, fresh, and expansive.

A *Divine Grace* orchestrates synchronicity and powers safe havens. An amazing protection cushions life's pathways. Auspicious happenings abound. Even apparent calamities bring forth some seemingly great fortune.

The *Presence* beams ever more bright, luminous, potent, as realized *Self*.

Spirit Is.

Divine Adoration of God Presence overflows in waterfalls of holy ecstatic devotion.

The depths of sacred surrender now arise as the only way to live or to be.

The Divine God Presence, as the beloved.

Intimate.

Holy.

Wild.

Tender.

Union.

Oneness.

Immense total reverence for and as God Presence.

Calm, anointed wisdom.

Behold: the holy power of the *Divinely Shattered Ones,* the *Safe Ones,* the *True Ones.*

The heart every instant humbly breaking open into radical surrender.

Sacredness Accepted

As Living Light

Father Ahavah!

Home in the Heart!

Still Home

Home

Selah!

Glossary of Terms

The definitions here offer pointers as to the meanings of words used in *Father Ahavah*. As many of these terms are ineffable and indescribable, this glossary represents the author's humble effort to clarify terms for the reader (similar to the humble effort of the entire book). The author does not claim to comprehensively define the undefinable.

Absolute
Synonym for God. The Absolute is that which is the Supreme Original Creator, The Original Light.

Adonai
Synonym for God. Adonai is a term for God or Lord used in the biblical texts. It is a word of the Hebrew language, in the Torah.

Ahavah

Hebrew word for Love, occurs in such sacred texts as the Bible, Torah, Nevi'im. It implies Divine Love, God's Love for his people. Jeremiah 31:3 "I have loved you with an everlasting love (Ahavah)." This Ahavah Presence is the Real. When we remember intimate Union with this Eternal Ahavah, and come alive as this Ahavah, the earth will turn golden in this reverence of, and Oneness with, Creator.

Bliss

Most used in this book as a synonym for God. Bliss describes the ecstatic holy intense joy of the Divine Presence. There is no true bliss apart from God union. Bliss is distinguished from the human "me" based happiness that depends upon avoiding pain and seeking pleasure. Bliss is not tied to any physical, emotional, or situational experience. It is causeless, "inner", eternal beingness.

Canticle

A sacred, holy, or spiritual song. I receive holy songs first as an invisible, ethereal essence or knowing. Then the canticle arises in the form of tones which I sound. Next a melody comes and then eventually words. These holy songs tend to have miraculous effects of spiritual realization and practical life healing for those who hear and experience them. To date, the canticles range from 30 seconds to fourteen minutes in length.

Divine Love

In this book, often used as a synonym for God; immense unconditional love that is beyond an emotion or feeling. It does not change, it is not subject to ups or downs, it is not given or withheld: It Is. God Presence, Eternal Spirit is the essence of Divine Love.

Divine Father

Synonym for God. The Divine Father describes the reverenced Father God, who intimately knows his child. Yet the Divine Father creates his child in oneness, in the same image and likeness— the Spirit Presence of Himself.

Divine Mother

Synonym for God. The Divine Mother describes the grace and compassion of our Holy Mother. This Holy Mother loves, nurtures, comforts, guides.

Divine Papa

Synonym for God and for Divine Father. This term describes an intimate closeness, an assurance of a loving union, an affectionate embracing union.

Essential Self

Synonym for Spirit Self, Spirit, or oneness with God Presence. The Essential Self is that which is essential. It is the true essence of what we exist as. The Essential Self we exist as does not change. It is of Spirit, Essence, the Presence. The non-essential self is that which changes and is temporary and that which can be dropped off and our core existence lives on. The non-essential self consists of thoughts, emotions, personality, relationships, situations—all of temporal life of a temporal life span.

Eternal Life Self

Synonym for oneness with God Presence; synonym for Spirit, Essential Self. The Eternal Life Self describes the life we exist as - as the Spirit Life that does not die. The Eternal Life Self does not begin after physical death. It is the reality we exist as now. Realization as Eternal Life Self dissolves the fear of death, which is the root of all other fears.

Father Ahavah

Synonym for God, for the Original Light of the Divine Presence. Father here denotes Father God. Ahavah in the Hebrew means Love. It denotes the Divine Love of God, the everlasting, unconditional Love. It is a synonym for True Existence: I Exist as One with Spirit, *Father Ahavah!* Father Ahavah denotes Father God Spirit, our Creator, from the most Original Absolute Beginning-Origin, the Living Light just Prior To, Father God.

God
The Eternal Creator. The Supreme Light, Love, Divine Intelligence. That Which is Above All Names, Nameless, Formless, The Totality. Yet the Nameless is given our best attempt at names such as the scriptural names: Ehyeh Asher Ehyeh, Yahweh, Elohim, Adonai, I AM.

Heaven
Heaven is not only referred to as a "place", a beingness we go to after physical death. Heaven is the Essence of God Presence, here, now. It denotes the Kingdom of God, the Reality of God Presence, wherein there is no suffering or pain. There exists total divine love, grace, beauty, completion, joy.

Holy One
Synonym for God. It denotes the most ineffable, worshipful, reverence for Creator and Oneness with that Creator as the Holy One.

Light
Synonym for God, Creator. The Supreme Being of all Luminous Glory. As Spirit, we exist as one with this Light, we exist as Light.

Living Light

Synonym for God. This term denotes and highlights that this God Light is Alive, it is Aliveness, it is the essence of Eternal, Immortal life. It is the Living Light that is not born and does not die, it does not change or decay or become ill. This Living Light is the Eternal Essence of God Presence.

Nameless One

Synonym for the Supreme Creator God. It denotes a sacred, reverent, worshipful awe. The Divine Presence is so sublime, holy, luminous that it is beyond all names and forms or any descriptions.

Natural Way

The Way of Spirit, of light, love, harmony, order, peace. It is the way of compassion, grace, Spirit inspiration. The Natural Way is the way of the Natural Self which is Spirit. It is before and beyond thoughts, perceptions, opinions, limitations, fear.

Original Light

Synonym for God. It is that which is Origin, before any form or names. The Original Light is Prior To any form—that which is pure, unalloyed, and free from all duality.

Personal "Me"

The identification with the name and form, the body and personality of this life span. It includes the beliefs, thoughts, emotions, and experiences of a separate sense of self, that feels and perceives itself to be separate from Creator. The personal "me" has hopes, desires, fears, wants, aversions, and is identified as a body that is born and dies. It is the named self, a separate sense of a "second self" in "addition" to Spirit Self. It is identified as the self, as "me", and as what existence is based upon. There may be a belief that when this personal "me" dies, then the self dies, or it disappears, or it goes on as this personal "me" in an afterlife. It is a "me" that is apart from Oneness with God. It is viewed as being born, suffering, experiencing personal ups and downs, pleasures and pains, and then ending in death.

Presence

Synonym for God. The Presence denotes the tangibly felt essence of Spirit. It may feel like lightness, peace, joy, expansion, sacredness. It has a more eternal and beautiful quality than the personal "me" contractions and limitations. God Presence—a felt reality of the essence of the Divine Love and Light.

Primordial

Synonym for Creator God. Primordial is akin to original —of the origin. The Light, Spirit, Presence unformed, timeless, infinite— before forms or births or persons or the world.

Primordial Self

Synonym for oneness with God, Light, the Original Spirit Presence. It is the Self that is Spirit, limitless, before and beyond suffering or lacks or limitations.

Pure Land

Similar to heaven or the kingdom of God. It is the nature, way and Light of God, Presence, Spirit. It is pure, before duality, before lacks or limitations. It is the sweet, ineffable, beauty of harmony, order, peace, oneness.

Quieting

The supreme, sublime stillness of God Presence. It is the Essence of God, when all sense of thought, emotion, personal "me" dissolves and the stillpoint of Light remains. It is the Original Self, an ineffable gentle, tender communion with and as God Spirit. The Quieting reveals a deep, abiding, pervading intimate love with God that is breathtaking in beauty.

Sacredness

What we exist as at our core essence: sacred. We exist as the sacredness, the holiness, the goodness, the innocence that is God Presence, God Light. There is no condemnation, rejection, badness, ineptness. It is the perfection and completion you exist as, as One with God Presence, that is eternally Sacred. Sacredness is the true essence reality of all things, all beings.

Self

Synonyn for God, or identification as One with God. It denotes identification - a point of identity as the true self- I Exist as One with God Presence.

Stillpoint

The Clear Light of God. Freedom from conflict, disturbance, duality. It is absolutely quiet, calm, unmoving, clear, total silence. Yet the still point silence has an aliveness as Light. It could form as anything, yet has no movement or "need" to form. Zero want, need, lack, or movement to create. It is all completion, deep pervading quiet.

Spirit Self

Identity as Spirit. The Self that is One with God Presence, that is eternal, infinite, ageless. Union with God, and aliveness as that union.

Softly Be

A phrase coined by the author that denotes a dissolving inwardly to any appearance, thought, emotion, personal "me" or "problem", while simultaneously "expanding out" to exist as Light. It is a total quiet, still power that is not a power over anyone or anything. It is the power of being the Presence, potently, in the face of any appearance. Being soft, tender, as potent God Presence.

True Life

True Life is the union with God Presence. It is Spirit Life, eternal life, that which denotes beauty, completion, fruition, fulfillment. There exists no separate sense of self, no separate "me". True Life is God Life, limitless freedom this instant.

The

End

and

The

Beginning

Thank You

From My Heart

For Honoring

Father Ahavah

Gratitude

Home in the Heart Mascot Rabbit: Bunny Ahavah —knew you'd be here, at the perfect moment for this book! You are pure golden Angel.

Congressman Bill Johnson: You exemplify the *Heart of the Father*. I appreciate your integrity and dedication to our Eternal Father. Thank you for your Presence in supporting this message reaching multitudes of hearts, across the globe. You are a true leader at a critical hour.

Guy King III: Thank you for your belief in this ministry and your support to usher the return of the *Heart of Father God Presence* upon the earth. Your charitable efforts support humanity coming to the true answer: Oneness with our Creator.

Nadina Fiveland: My beautiful eternal friend, I treasure your heart-felt zeal for this book, *Father Ahavah*.

The Property—My Sweet home—we shared the joy of beauty and service, in the long hours of the day and working through the night, as one, offering this to the humans, and all life in all realms, rested in ecstatic adoration in Father Ahavah Presence.

Debbie Loshbough—Copy Editor and Final Edits: You honored this book, *Father Ahavah*, with your gracious service, freely offered from your heart. Your second pair of eyes did a fantastic job with the final edits. You filled an unexpected need, quickly, with a commitment to service for all beings.

Joanne Hill: You stepped into the delivery room right at the moment of birth—celebrating the *Father Ahavah* message, and a forerunner in seeing the vision of this book's impact.

George Felos: You reveal the *Heart of the Father*, and compassion. Your caring contemplation of the book brought forth the subtitle idea, the *Unfathered Ones*... and the talk that inspired Chapter 18, giving birth.

Bob Houston, Interior Graphic Designer: You are a joy to work with, engaged with *Father Ahavah*, going above and beyond. I love the Hebrew glyph. Dr. Ellipse...

Cassie Marie Franek—Book Cover Artist: You maintained a wonderfully responsive flow to our creative process. Beautiful!

Home In The Heart Foundation

homeintheheartfoundation.com

Ann Marie Nielsen, Ph.D.

drannmarie.com

Online Classroom

homeintheheart.com

We Welcome You to Join

Home in the Heart

Family

Still Home

Home

אגדה

Made in the USA
Lexington, KY
27 April 2016